SECOND TO NONE

SECOND TO NONE

A PICTORIAL HISTORY OF HORNCHURCH AERODROME THROUGH TWO WORLD WARS AND BEYOND, 1915–1962

Richard C. Smith

GRUB STREET • LONDON

Published by
Grub Street
4 Rainham Close
London
SW11 6SS

Copyright © 2004 Grub Street
Text copyright © 2004 Richard C. Smith

British Library Cataloguing in Publication Data
Smith, Richard C., 1956-
    Second to none: a pictorial history of Hornchurch
    Aerodrome through two World Wars and beyond, 1915-1962:
    Zeppelin raids, Dunkirk, Battle of Britain, Dieppe,
    European offensive
    1.RAF Hornchurch - History 2.RAF Hornchurch - History -
    Pictorial works
    I.Title
    358.4'17'094217

    ISBN 1 904010 78 4

Typeset by Eclipse, Hemel Hempstead

Printed and bound by Bookprint, Spain

CONTENTS

DEDICATIONS

This book is dedicated to the memory of two fine gentlemen, Mr Ted Exall (left) and Mr Ken Finding, who during their lives helped to bring the history of RAF Hornchurch to thousands of others who wished to know more.

This book is also dedicated to Squadron Leader Peter Brown, AFC RAF Retd, 'One of the Few'. Peter's help over the years in matters of historical reference pertaining to the Royal Air Force and the Battle of Britain, has not only given us many hours of enjoyable experiences together, but has made us great friends. Thank you.

ACKNOWLEDGEMENTS

The author would like to thank the following men, women, museums and institutions listed below, for without their help this book would not have been possible. Sadly so many of these fine people have now passed on. We will never see their like again.

Flight Lieutenant William 'Tex' Ash MBE
The late Squadron Leader Robert Beardsley DFC
The late Air Commodore Ronald Berry OBE, DSO, DFC
The late Air Chief Marshal Sir Harry Broadhurst GCB, KBE, DSO, DFC
Squadron Leader Peter Brown AFC, RAF Retd
The late Air Commodore Alan Deere, DSO, OBE, DFC
The late Squadron Leader Dave Glaser DFC
The late Group Captain Colin Gray DSO, DFC
The late Flight Lieutenant Leslie Harvey
The late Sgt P. S. Hayes
Group Captain D.S. 'Sammy' Hoare RAF Retd
Squadron Leader Arthur Leigh DFC, DFM, RAF Retd
The late Squadron Leader Peter Morfill DFM
The late Wing Commander Tom Rowland
The late Wing Commander Gerald Saunders DFC
The late Air Vice-Marshal David Scott-Malden DSO, DFC
Air Marshal Sir Frederick Sowrey KCB, CBE, AFC, RAF Retd
The late Wing Commander H. M. Stephen CBE, DSO, DFC, AE
Mr Robert Ballard
Mr David Bendon
Mr Harold Bennett
Mrs Jessica Berryman
Lady Dorothy Bouchier
Mr Leslie Bruce
Mr Harry Bullock
Mr Joe Crawshaw – Chairman of 222 Natal Squadron
Mrs Joy Caldwell
Mr John Cox
Mr Frank Decmar
Mr Barrie Green
Mr John Hewitt
Mr Danny Kilgariff
Mr Howard La Roche
Mr Roy Little
Mr Frank Mileham
Mr Anthony Philpot
Mr David Ross
Mr Andy Saunders
Mr Howard Squire
Mr Michael Taylor

2048 Dagenham Squadron Air Training Corps Archive
The Air Historical Branch, Bentley Priory
The London Borough of Havering Library Services
The Photographic Archive at the Imperial War Museum and its staff
The Keystone Press
The National Archive
The Purfleet Heritage and Military Centre – Hornchurch Wing Collection
The Royal Air Force Museum, Photographic Archive, Hendon
The RAF Hornchurch Association Collection
Sports and General Press Ltd

Thanks again to all my family, friends and aviation associates, and to the members of the public who buy the books and turn up for the book launches and give great encouragement. Thank you to John Davies and all at Grub Street who continue to 'Keep the Faith' and produce outstanding books.

INTRODUCTION

This is the history of one of the Royal Air Force's most famous Fighter Command aerodromes, which initially came to prominence during the First World War, when the Zeppelin airship raids were causing terrified civilians to seek shelter from the first aerial bombing to be used in modern warfare.

The small airfield then known as Sutton's Farm, Hornchurch, was where the first primitive aircraft of the Royal Flying Corps met the challenge, and became the new knights of the air.

Hornchurch proved itself again in the Second World War, when the young men of the Royal Air Force, and particularly those serving at the aerodrome, bested the Luftwaffe bomber and fighter hordes, that threatened British skies during the Battle of Britain.

This pictorial tome takes you through the entire 47-year history of RAF Hornchurch, showing you the men and women, who served and fought so valiantly in wartime as well as continuing to uphold the tradition of the Royal Air Force during peacetime.

The continuing advance of aircraft technology is also covered in this book, from the early fabric and wooden biplanes of WW1 up until the monoplanes of the 1950s.

It is often said that 'a picture or photograph can say a thousand words,' and certainly the photographs in this book capture the essence and spirit of those who lived from day to day, hour to hour during wartime. Many of the people featured were killed or injured in action, maybe minutes, hours or days after the photograph had been taken, which therefore became the last recorded evidence of their life.

The photographs have been drawn from a wide selection of sources, some from pilot's and ground personnel's own private albums taken during informal situations, others by professional press photographers called to the aerodrome to record an event of significance. All are equally important images of history.

I hope this book will leave the reader with one thought above all, that they can be justly proud of the men and women of the Royal Air Force, who have served their country for the last 86 years and continue to do so today.

Richard C. Smith
June 2004

CHAPTER 1
SUTTON'S FARM
1915 – 1919

At the outbreak of the First World War in August 1914, the small country village of Hornchurch, 15 miles from the centre of London, was totally unaware that within a few short years it would become a centre of attention, when a new form of warfare would appear and become predominant.

In Germany airships had been developed over many years; their greatest pioneer in this field being Count Ferdinand von Zeppelin. The new airships now named after Zeppelin, had the capacity to travel large distances over land and sea and also deliver bombs against an enemy. At the beginning of January 1915, the German naval command who operated the Zeppelins were given the authority to bomb Britain, but it was firmly stipulated in the beginning that only military targets were to be attacked. This would not remain the case.

The new German menace first arrived over Britain on the night of 19th/20th January 1915, when two airships, LZ.3 and LZ.4 dropped bombs on Sheringham, Snettisham, King's Lynn and Yarmouth in Norfolk. Casualties on the ground were four killed and

16 injured, but the effect it had on the British civilian population was to be more significant. No longer were the British safe from the enemy across the Channel, protected by 20 miles of water, which had seen the likes of the Spanish Armada and Napoleon Bonaparte stopped in their tracks, centuries before.

To defend against these attacks the War Ministry looked for suitable landing grounds from which the embryo Royal Flying Corps could operate and take off to try and engage the German gargantuan of the air. One such site was Sutton's Farm, owned by New College Oxford and farmed by Tom Crawford. His farmland consisted of 90 acres of fields that were flat and well drained. After inspection by officials and Royal Flying Corps officers, part of the land was deemed suitable for military use and was officially requisitioned.

On 3rd October 1915, the Royal Flying Corps arrived by truck at Sutton's Farm, a group consisting of one officer, Captain A.G. Moore, and 12 men from 23 Squadron. They immediately began to erect bell tents for accommodation and two canvas hangars and began unloading the aviation fuel, armament and other supplies required to make the landing ground operational. Later during that day, two BE2c biplanes arrived from Gosport from 13 Squadron of 5 Wing. The pilots were billeted in the local White Hart public house in Hornchurch village, while the ground staff slept at one of the local farmhouses.

The first action against the enemy was not long in coming however, when on the night of 13th October, the Germans launched their largest raid of the war to date. Five Zeppelins had left their moorings at Nordholz in northern Germany and headed across the North Sea, four of them making landfall over the Norfolk and Suffolk coasts, while Zeppelin L.15 was sighted at 8.00 pm over Halstead, Essex, turning south-west for London. After dropping her bomb load and causing the deaths of 72 civilians and many more injured, the airship headed back for Germany. With the local air defences alerted, Sutton's Farm received a telephone communication to bring them at once in to the action.

A young 18-year-old pilot, Lieutenant John Slessor was ordered aloft immediately in his biplane at 9.05 pm and began the 40-minute climb to an altitude of 10,000 feet in order to intercept the raider. Slessor caught up with the giant airship, locked in the beams of the searchlight batteries below, but as he approached to make his attack, the airship disappeared in to a cloudbank and he never found it again. This had been Slessor's first operational patrol and he is now recorded as being the first British pilot to intercept an enemy airship over Britain.

Success against the German airship raids finally came on the night of 2nd/3rd September 1916, when Second Lieutenant William Leefe Robinson based at Sutton's Farm with 39 'Home Defence' Squadron was called into action to tackle the German Army airship, Schutte-Lanz SL.11 which had been reported over Hertfordshire, on its approach to London. Taking off at 11.08 pm, Robinson was ordered to patrol between Sutton's Farm and Joyce Green. It was not until 1.10 am that he caught sight of SL.11, trapped in the glare of the searchlights. After following the airship's path, Robinson lost sight of the craft when it went into cloud, and it was to be another 15 minutes before he was able to find the enemy, which was silhouetted against the searchlights over north-east London. He attacked at a height of 11,500 feet, flying 800 feet below the German giant, firing his machine guns from bow to stern as he went. Finally after a second attack, Robinson noticed a red glow appear and soon the airship was ablaze and falling from the sky. The crew stood no chance and all perished, SL.11 finally crashing down to earth at Cuffley, Hertfordshire.

The spectacle of the German airship alight had been seen by many civilians from Staines to Southend and a great cry had gone up as the giant ball of flame lit up the night sky. The Germans no longer seemed invincible. William Leefe Robinson had become a national hero overnight and Sutton's Farm, Hornchurch was now in the headlines.

On 5th September, Robinson was awarded the Victoria Cross by King George V at Windsor Castle; meanwhile the people of Hornchurch basked in their new-found fame and referred to 'our aerodrome' as visitors made frequent visits to view and catch a glimpse of the officers and men of the Royal Flying Corps. Within the space of a month, two further airships would fall prey to the guns of pilots from Sutton's Farm.

On 23rd/24th September, Lieutenant Frederick Sowrey brought down Zeppelin

LZ.32 near Billericay, while Lieutenant Wulstan Tempest destroyed LZ.31 on the night of 1st/2nd October, forcing it to crash at Potters Bar. Both Sowrey and Tempest were awarded the Distinguished Service Order.

A new menace was looming however, with the arrival of newly developed German biplane bombers, which had the capacity to fly over London; these were the twin-engine Gotha and the LVG CII reconnaissance aircraft. The first raid against London was made on 28th November 1916. In late June of 1917, 39 Squadron received new aircraft to replace their BE12s and were allocated the new Sopwith Pup fighter, which was faster and better armed to deal with the Gotha threat. Another new squadron, 46, was sent to the airfield on 10th July 1917, ordered back from France to help repel the Gotha raids. But the squadron's stay was brief and the pilots were returned to France in the August. During September 1917, 39 Squadron was posted to North Weald and its place was taken by 78 Squadron. The squadron was equipped at that time with the Sopwith 1½ Strutter, but soon after this was replaced with the new Sopwith Camel. It was also during the month of September that women in uniform were first seen arriving at the airfield. The ladies of the newly formed Women's Legion Auxiliary were sent to work alongside the men as telephonists, clerical staff and drivers. Many were billeted in the large country-style house at Bretton's Farm, which was situated between the airfield and Dagenham, and which still stands today.

At the beginning of March 1918, Sutton's Farm was allotted the task of giving flight demonstrations of the RFC's latest aircraft, which would succeed the Sopwith Camel. The new prototype biplane, named the Sopwith Snipe, was shown off to high-ranking officers and officials by ace pilot Captain James McCudden VC, who gave a thrilling display showing its great manoeuvrability.

On 1st April 1918, the Royal Flying Corps was changed in name to the Royal Air Force and at Sutton's Farm another squadron, 189 Night-Training Squadron arrived to take up its position alongside 78. The airfield was now under the command of 49 Wing, whose headquarters were housed at Upminster Hall; its commander was Colonel Malcolm G. Christie, who was married to the famous authoress Agatha Christie.

At the close of war on 11th November 1918, 300 RAF officers and men and 24 WRAFs staffed the airfield, but soon after the closure of hostilities, it was decided by the War Office that Sutton's Farm would be of no further use in the future. The remaining squadrons were therefore disbanded, 189 on 31st March 1919 and 78 Squadron on 31st December.

The land was given back to farmer Tom Crawford, the wooden huts and the hangars were torn down, but some of the brick buildings were left standing and used for agricultural purposes. So ended the short life of one of this country's outstanding airfields of the First World War, where heroic deeds had taken place and had secured in memory the names of men who had risked their lives in flimsy aircraft at night, with no navigational aids or communication assistance, but who had dealt a huge blow to an enemy trying to break the will of the British civilian population through bombing their cities. It could be said that this was the first 'Battle of Britain'. Twenty-four years later the next Battle of Britain would be more deadly and with more dire consequences.

Top: The White Hart Public House located in the centre of Hornchurch village. It was here that the first Royal Flying Corps pilots were billeted in October 1915. *(The London Borough of Havering Library Service)*

Bottom: Early aviation was extremely risqué, as is demonstrated in this photograph showing a BE2c biplane which has nosed in whilst landing. The aircraft 4110 was used by 19 Flying Reserve Squadron at Sutton's Farm and was flown by Lieutenant William Leefe Robinson on 4th February 1916. Robinson is pictured with the damaged aircraft although it is not known if he was flying it when the accident occurred. *(RAF Museum)*

Top: Three pilot friends of 39 (Home Defence) Squadron pictured walking arm in arm at Sutton's Farm. Left to right: Lieutenants Wulstan Tempest, Leefe Robinson and Frederick Sowrey. Note the farm building behind and wooden hangar on left. *(F. Sowrey)*

Bottom: Lieutenant Robinson is pictured in the cockpit of his BE2c biplane, serial number 2693 in which he shot down the Schutte–Lanz airship SL.11 on the night of 2nd/3rd September 1916 and was awarded the Victoria Cross. His ground crew stand with part of the aircraft's centre section of the top wing, which Robinson had damaged during the action. *(F. Sowrey)*

Top: A postcard of the period depicts the German airship's final moments on 3rd September 1916. *(Author)*

Bottom: A photograph showing the amazing length of German Zeppelin L.32. At 650 feet it was an awesome sight to behold viewed from the ground as well as from the air. *(Author)*

Opposite page: VC winner William Leefe Robinson poses for the camera in leafy Sutton's Lane, Hornchurch, September 1916. *(Luff)*

THE ZEPPELIN'S DIVE TO DEATH
SUNDAY SEPT 3rd 1916.

Top: Some of the officers of 39 Squadron beside Lieutenant Frederick Sowrey's aircraft parked outside the wooden hangars, following his successful attack the night previous on Zeppelin L.32, which crashed at Great Berstead, Billericay on 24th September 1916. Left to right: Lieutenants Mallinson and Tempest, Captain Bowers, Sowrey and Lieutenant Durstan. *(F. Sowrey)*

Bottom left: A ground crewman of the Royal Flying Corps stands within the bomb crater of a bomb that was dropped on Sutton's Farm airfield by Zeppelin L.32 on the previous night of 23rd September 1916. *(The London Borough of Havering Library Service)*

Bottom right: A defused German bomb of the type that was dropped from the Zeppelin airships over London during 1915/16. *(Author)*

Top: William Leefe Robinson is presented with his silver trophy cup at the New Zealand Army Camp at Grey Towers Mansion, Hornchurch on 14th October 1916. It was given to him for shooting down the German airship SL.11. The trophy cup was one of three, which were awarded to the pilots of Sutton's Farm in 1916. The trophies were paid for with monies raised by the residents of the Parish of Hornchurch. *(Luff)*

Bottom: Another view taken at the presentation of the silver cups to the three Zeppelin heroes. Note the New Zealand flag in full prominence. Frederick Sowrey can be seen seated above between the trophies. The Grey Towers Camp was used as the headquarters of the New Zealand Soldiers' Convalescent Hospital in 1916. *(London Borough of Havering Library Service)*

Top left: A good study of the different Royal Flying Corps uniforms worn at the time, showing, left to right Lieutenants Sowrey, Robinson and Captain Stammers. Robinson is wearing the wrap over jacket, known as a maternity tunic. *(F. Sowrey)*

Top right: Robinson and Sowrey pictured driving down Sutton's Lane. *(F. Sowrey)*

Bottom left: An informal group photograph of Royal Flying Corps officers of 46 Squadron relaxing outside one of the huts at Sutton's Farm in August 1917.
(The RAF Museum)

Bottom right: Promoted to the rank of Captain, William Robinson is presented with a gift from the children of St Leonard's Cottage Homes in Hornchurch. *(London Borough of Havering Library Services)*

Top left: An unidentified officer of 46 Squadron pictured next to one of the corrugated buildings at Sutton's in 1917. *(The RAF Museum)*

Top right: 'Anyone for tennis'. An officer of 46 Squadron poses for the camera wearing his tennis trousers and shoes. Behind him stands one of the wooden huts built with a raised brick foundation. *(The RAF Museum)*

Bottom: Ground personnel of 78 Squadron pictured in front of a FE2d pusher-biplane at Sutton's in September 1917. These aircraft were replaced by Sopwith 1½ Strutters in October. *(The RAF Museum)*

Top: Another view of one of the two FE2d aircraft used by 78 Squadron. This is B1883. These machines had the engine and propeller mounted behind the pilot's cockpit, while the gunner or observer was seated up front in the nose section. *(J.M. Bruce-S. Leslie Collection)*

Middle: Sopwith 1½ Strutter A6906 '5' of 78 Squadron is pushed back to the hangars. *(The RAF Museum)*

Bottom left: Lieutenant David Greswolde Lewis of 78 Squadron stands with his Sopwith Camel named 'Rhodesia'. After serving with 78 Squadron, Lewis was posted to France to 3 Squadron on 29th March 1918. On 20th April, he became the last victim of Manfred von Richthofen, the Red Baron. Lewis was flying Sopwith Camel B7393 when Richthofen attacked him and his aircraft was set alight north-east of Villers-Bretonneux at 6.43 pm. Fortunately Lewis survived the crash landing and spent the remainder of the war as a prisoner. *(The RAF Museum)*

Bottom right: Two unidentified officers of 78 Squadron seen pictured at a waterlogged and muddy Sutton's Farm during the winter of 1917. Note the substantial brick farm buildings behind the wooden huts. *(The RAF Museum)*

Top left: Captain D.V. Armstrong of 78 Squadron. He engaged a German Gotha biplane bomber on 19th May 1918, near Orsett, Essex. The combat lasted 20 minutes, before Armstrong broke away. The German was eventually brought down by a Bristol Fighter of 39 Squadron and crashed at Roman Road, East Ham. *(Author)*

Top right: Captain Douglas John Bell of 78 Squadron pictured next to the motor transport at Sutton's in 1917. On the evening of 25th September 1917, Bell accompanied by 2nd Lieutenant G.G. Williams in a Sopwith 1½ Strutter, managed to intercept and attack a German Gotha bomber south of Brentwood, Essex. After their attack they unfortunately lost sight of the aircraft, but the Gotha apparently ditched in the North Sea. Bell was credited with 20 victories before he was killed on 27th May 1918. *(The RAF Museum)*

Bottom: Sopwith Camel B3803 on a visit to Sutton's Farm stands ready to take to the air. This aircraft was used for training and was stationed at the Central Flying School at Upavon, before it crashed on 17th November 1917, killing the pilot. *(The RAF Museum)*

Top: A group photograph of officers of 78 Squadron at Sutton's Farm in 1918 with one of their Sopwith Camel aircraft pictured behind. *(The RAF Museum)*

Bottom left: Forerunners of the Women's Auxiliary Air Force, ladies of the Women's Legion Auxiliary at Sutton's Farm 1917/18. Miss Grace Hewitson is pictured centre. *(Crabtree)*

Bottom right: Two young ladies of the Women's Legion Auxiliary are photographed in one of the wooden hut offices at Sutton's Farm in 1918. Miss Grace Hewitson is pictured on the right. *(Crabtree)*

Top: Bretton's Farm Country House, where members of the Women's Legion Auxiliary were billeted during this period. Some of the young ladies felt uneasy, when they were told of rumours that the building was haunted. *(Author)*

Bottom: A Sopwith Pup biplane, serial number 312 of 189 Night Training Squadron, Sutton's Farm 1918. Note the elaborate paintwork on the fuselage depicting stars. *(L. Bruce)*

This page: Two excellent views of an SE 5A biplane, serial number B554 during 1918.

The second photograph shows the prefabricated hangars that were being used at this time. *(The RAF Museum)*

Top: An officer of the Royal Navy Air Service inspects the cockpit of Sopwith Snipe E8076 belonging to 78 Squadron, 1918. *(L. Bruce)*

Bottom: Invited members of the public are treated to the first public demonstration of air-to-ground wireless telephony by 141 Squadron at the airfield in 1918.

CHAPTER 2

RAF HORNCHURCH:
THE INTER-WAR YEARS
1928 - 1939

In 1922, the Royal Air Force's Chief of Air Staff Lord Hugh Trenchard, together with a committee which included the Secretary of State for Air, Sir Samuel Hoare and the Marquis of Salisbury, had put forward a report which discussed the expansion of the air force and what role the service would play alongside the other armed forces. Included within this report was the creation of home defence squadrons. The final paper was submitted to Parliament that year and its findings concluded that the Government should make provision for 14 bomber and nine fighter squadrons. With this increase in the air force there would also be the need for new airfields to operate from.

During the latter part of 1922, former World War One airfields were investigated by the Air Ministry to see if they were suitable for use once again and Sutton's Farm, Hornchurch was visited and inspected on 24th November 1922.

The conclusion of the inspection party was that Sutton's Farm was suitable, but it would be too small for the proposed airfield and that the land further south would also have to be purchased to enlarge the area further, if a new site was to be built. They reckoned that the position of the new airfield was ideal however, because of its strategic strength in covering enemy attacks into London following the path of the Thames estuary.

A contract with the landowners New College, Oxford for the sale of Sutton's Farm, was agreed and signed in July 1923, which left farmer Tom Crawford who still worked the land, very little area to continue his livelihood.

Construction of the new airfield did not start until May 1924 and it was not until 1st April 1928, that the airfield was officially opened. It was initially re-named RAF Sutton's Farm, but two months later the name was changed to RAF Hornchurch.

The new airfield did not start life with an overall commanding officer; the role of officer in charge was given to the first squadron commander, Squadron Leader Keith Park. Park flew down from RAF Duxford with his squadron, 111, who were equipped with Armstrong Whitworth Siskin biplanes. The following month of June saw the arrival of General Italo Balbo, the famous Italian aviator; he was the first of many VIPs who would visit the aerodrome over the next 30 years.

During March 1929, the airfield was assigned its first official station commander, Squadron Leader F.O. Soden. During April and May, the aircrew were involved with anti-aircraft and army co-operation exercises. During July, two further squadrons on detachment joined 111 Squadron, 19 flying in from RAF Duxford, while 23 Squadron flying Gloster Gamecocks arrived from Kenley.

At the beginning of January 1930, 19 and 23 Squadrons had departed and 54 Squadron, operating with Siskin aircraft during this time, filled their place. Four days after their arrival the squadron converted to the new Bristol Bulldog biplane. This squadron would become a mainstay at Hornchurch for years to come and achieve many plaudits.

The routine at Hornchurch over the next few years was fairly ordinary, apart from carrying out air defence exercises or preparing for air displays, such as the Hendon Air Pageant or the Empire Air Day. The squadrons remained the same until 12th July 1934, when 111 was posted to RAF Northolt and was replaced by a newly re-formed 65 Squadron, flying Hawker Demon aircraft.

In 1935, the aerodrome played host to two visiting VIPs, when the Air Officer Commander-in-Chief Air Defence of Great Britain, Air Vice-Marshal Sir Robert Brooke-Popham arrived with Sir Philip Sassoon. The annual Empire Air Display held in May of that year was an outstanding success, with an attendance of 4,500, which raised £163, a very large sum of money in those days.

Hornchurch was asked to play host for the 1936 Air Defence of Great Britain held in March that year. Over the week of the exercises, various squadrons took part in defending and attacking given targets, which included the Ford motor factory at Dagenham, situated a few miles south of the airfield on the banks of the Thames. Hornchurch squadrons were given the task of defending the targets.

The sport-minded servicemen of RAF Hornchurch won the Air Council Cup and the RAF Athletics Championship in June that year and one pilot officer named Donald Finlay, who was an outstanding athlete, was chosen to captain the British Olympic team who would participate in the games held in Munich, Germany, later that year.

Another squadron took up residence at Hornchurch in September 1936; this was 74 Squadron, the famous World War One fighter unit. It had disbanded after the war and had reformed in Malta in 1935. Its commanding officer was Squadron Leader Donald Brookes, and soon after arriving, a new pilot officer came to take up his role within the squadron. He would later become one of the RAF's most famous wartime commanders - Adolph Gysbert Malan, nicknamed 'Sailor' because of his previous time in the Merchant Navy.

By late 1936, the airfield's status was raised to that of Sector Station 'D' in the new 11 Group area, which covered the defence of London and the south-east. The Commander-in-Chief of Fighter Command, Air Chief Marshal Hugh Dowding arrived at Hornchurch at this time and inspected the newly built operations room in its underground block, which was installed with the latest technology for ground-to-air control and the new radio direction finding equipment, which was still being tested at this time.

In the April of 1937, both 54 and 65 Squadrons had replaced their Gloster Gauntlet aircraft with the new Gloster Gladiator, the first RAF fighter to have a fully enclosed cockpit. That same month, 74 Squadron exchanged its two-seater Hawker Demons for single-seat Gauntlets. This meant that aircrew gunners were now surplus to requirement and many of the men were posted to other units or retrained as ground crew.

It was also during this year that Hornchurch was visited by a German delegation which consisted of high-ranking Luftwaffe officers, who included General Erhard Milch and Ernst Udet. They were given a full tour of the station, which included a full inspection of the Gloster Gladiators and the new reflector gun-sight, which was only just coming into service. The pilots of 65 Squadron had been given strict instructions not to talk to the Germans on the workings of the new gun-sight, so when General Milch approached Flying Officer Robert Stanford Tuck to discuss its operation, Tuck said he was unable to help. At that very moment an RAF air vice-marshal interrupted proceedings and gave the general a full run down on the new instrument, while a shocked Bob Tuck looked on.

During the year of 1938, Hornchurch was again host to many visitors including the famous woman aviator Jean Batten, who had flown solo halfway around the world in her Percival Gull monoplane. Throughout this period a number of new officers were sent to Hornchurch to take up postings to their first squadrons. Many would become renowned pilots during the Battle of Britain; Brian Kingcome and Alan Deere were just two of them.

In September 1938, Hornchurch along with many other airfields, was put on a full war alert because of the serious situation which had arisen in Europe due to Adolf Hitler's claims for land in the Sudeten region of Czechoslovakia. Known as the Munich Crisis, the outbreak of another war was thankfully averted, when an agreement was brokered by Britain and France, to hand over the Sudetenland to Germany. It was hoped at the time that this would avert Herr Hitler from any further thoughts of German expansion.

At Hornchurch, during this crisis, the squadrons had for the first time been ordered to camouflage their aircraft. All the available paint was brought out from the stores and the beautiful silver biplanes were unceremoniously covered in brown and green. Unfortunately there was not enough paint to cover all the aircraft, so teams of ground crew were ordered to the local shops to buy up whatever was available. They set about mixing various colours to resemble brown and green and these were applied with old brushes, brooms and pieces of rags. The aircraft looked terrible with their varying colour schemes for a few weeks after, until the proper paint was brought in to do the job properly.

On a different note, on November 25th, 74 Squadron's team of pilots won the Sir Philip Sassoon Challenge Trophy, which was held at RAF Northolt that year. As 1939 approached, the squadrons were informed that within the next couple of months, some of the fighter squadrons within the Royal Air Force would be re-equipped with the new eight-gun monoplane aircraft, the Supermarine Spitfire.

The first squadron at Hornchurch to receive the new aircraft was, 74, and the first example of this was flown into Hornchurch on 13th February 1939 by Squadron Leader D.S. Brookes. The aircraft was Spitfire Mk 1, serial no. K9860. The next squadron to receive Spitfires was 54; Flight Lieutenant James Leathart collected its initial aircraft from Eastleigh on 3rd March, flying K9880.

65 Squadron was last in receiving the new aircraft, when Flight Lieutenant A.N. Jones collected its first Spitfire on 21st March 1939. Hornchurch would become the only completely Spitfire-based airfield throughout the Battle of Britain in 1940.

In May, the aerodrome hosted its last Empire Air Day, which attracted a huge gathering of 45,000 people. During the day the famous air-racing pilot Alex Henshaw arrived in his record-breaking Mew Gull aircraft to sign autographs for an enthusiastic crowd. Henshaw would later be one of Vickers Supermarine's test pilots during WW2.

Meanwhile the situation on the European mainland had worsened to such a degree that on 22nd August once again Hornchurch along with other aerodromes was put on an immediate war footing. On 1st September 1939, despite numerous warnings, Germany continued its aggression and threats of expansion and invaded Poland. Two days later on 3rd September after refusing the ultimatum given by Britain and France for Nazi Germany to back down, the two countries declared war.

Fortunately for the pilots of Fighter Command, the year's grace following the Munich Crisis had given the country the breathing space and time to build more of the new Hurricanes and Spitfires and allowed the pilots precious flying hours to train and get to know the capabilities of their aircraft. Many of the pilots then stationed at Hornchurch would make names for themselves and become aces in the forthcoming conflict, men such as John Mungo-Park, John Freeborn, Bill Franklin, George Gribble and Johnny Allen.

Top: The entrance to the newly built RAF Hornchurch aerodrome in 1928, with RAF guard on duty. The building on the left is the Guard Room. *(RAF Hornchurch Association)*

Middle: Another view taken in 1928, showing some of the blockhouse buildings within the airfield perimeter fence looking in from the South End Road. *(RAF Hornchurch Association)*

Bottom: The newly built and impressive Officers' Mess with further quarters situated either side. The Mess was located across the South End Road from the main station. *(RAF Hornchurch Association)*

Hornchurch Aerodrome.

The Hangers, Hornchurch Aerodrome.

Top and Middle: These two photographs show the C-type hangars that were built at Hornchurch with the Watch Office located in front with windsock. *(RAF Hornchurch Association)*

Bottom: An Armstrong Whitworth Siskin belonging to RAF Hornchurch's first operational squadron, 111, is prepared for take-off in 1928. *(The RAF Museum)*

Top: Italian aviator General Italo Balbo (centre), Commander-in Chief of the Regia Aeronautica (Italian Air Force) arrived at Hornchurch with other Italian aviators to represent Italy in the RAF pageant at Hendon in June 1928. Pictured with Balbo are (left) Air Vice-Marshal Scarlett of Schneider Cup fame and Italian flying officer Captain Manghi. *(Author)*

Bottom: In early 1931 111 Squadron replaced its old Siskin biplanes with the new Bristol Bulldog. One of the new aircraft stands parked just off the concrete apron in front of the main hangar. *(The RAF Museum)*

Top: An excellent aerial photograph of a
Bristol Bulldog serving with 54 Squadron
in 1932. *(Air Historical Branch)*

Bottom: A Hawker Audax belonging to an army co-operation unit,
pictured at Hornchurch in 1934. The aircraft has parked next to the
aerodrome's compass circle, where the aircraft's compass could be set
and re-aligned. *(The RAF Museum)*

Top: Smoke on! Bristol Bulldogs of 54 Squadron practice their routine ready for the annual Empire Air Day. Below is the River Thames with the Ford Motor Company just visible on far left of photograph. May 1936. *(Author)*

Bottom: A squadron group photograph showing officers and ground personnel of 74 Squadron in October 1936. *(The RAF Museum)*

Top: A visiting Hawker Fury (K1930) is inspected by fellow officers at Hornchurch. *(The RAF Museum)*

Bottom: Three Gloster Gauntlets of 65 Squadron's aerobatic team –November 1936. *(Author)*

Squadron Leader Cecil 'Boy' Bouchier, commander of 54 Squadron (2nd from left) is pictured in front of one of the squadron's Gauntlet aircraft in 1936. With him are P.E. Warcup on left and R.C. Love on right. Gentleman in white overalls is unknown. *(C. Bouchier)*

Top: Officers of
B Flight 65 Squadron
line up in front of a
Gauntlet biplane in
March 1937. Left to
right: Unknown,
G. Saunders,
L. Bicknall, S/Ldr
D. Cooke, R.S. Tuck,
A. Hope-Boyd,
H. Giddings and
G. Proudman.
(G. Saunders)

Bottom: A visiting
Hawker Super
Fury biplane at
Hornchurch in 1937.
(D.S. Hoare)

Top: Outside the Watch Office in 1937 are three of 65 Squadron's young pilot officers. Robert Stanford Tuck, Jack Kennedy and John Welford. *(G. Saunders)*

Bottom: A Vickers Virginia MkX bomber biplane pictured while visiting the aerodrome in 1937. Note the ground personnel seeking shade under the aircraft's giant wings. *(Sgt P.S. Hayes)*

Top left: The shattered and buried wreckage of Gloster Gauntlet K7828 of 65 Squadron with its rudder still intact, lies within the Maylands aerodrome at Harold Wood, near Romford, after crashing on 25th May 1937. The aircraft flown by Sergeant Frederick Boxall had been performing aerobatics at 2,000 feet, when part of the top starboard wing broke away. The aircraft went into an uncontrollable spin and crashed in to the ground killing its pilot. *(P. Morfill)*

Top right: Frederick William Boxall, who was tragically killed while performing aerobatics, aged 21 years. He had been attached to 65 Squadron from 74 Squadron also based at Hornchurch. *(A. Philpot)*

Bottom: Ground personnel manoeuvre a Gloster Gauntlet II of 65 Squadron into position out on to the aerodrome in 1937. *(Author)*

Top: Inside one of the hangars at Hornchurch in 1937, an engine fitter works on a 74 'Tiger' Squadron Gloster Gauntlet. *(D.S. Hoare)*

Bottom: RAF ground personnel pictured during the Home Defence Exercise carried out on 13th August 1937. The men carry practice bombs while wearing a gas mask in the summer heat. The aircraft is a Fairey Gordon of 6 Squadron, which operated from the aerodrome during the exercise. *(Author)*

Top: Lined up outside the hangars, ready for inspection are Gloster Gauntlets of 65 (F) Squadron in 1937. *(Author)*

Bottom: On 17th January 1938, two Gloster Gladiators of 65 Squadron collided whilst practising aerobatics. Flying Officer Robert Stanford Tuck baled out injured, but Sergeant Gaskill was killed in the collision. The aircraft, K7940 and K8014, both crashed near Uckfield, Sussex. The photograph shows the wreckage of Tuck's aircraft, surrounded by civilians at the crash-site. *(A. Saunders)*

Top: The Sultan of Muscat visited Hornchurch on 31st March 1938 during his state visit to London. Here he is seen inspecting the men and Gladiator aircraft of 65 Squadron. *(G. Saunders)*

Bottom: Pilots of B Flight, 65 Squadron with ground personnel in 1938. Pilots seated second row left to right are: Sgt Winterbottom, ?, Adrian Hope-Boyd, Gerald Saunders, Leslie Bicknall, Robert Stanford Tuck, Herbert Giddings, George Proudman and Sgt Percy Morfill. *(G. Saunders)*

Top: Members of the public inspect a Hawker Hind biplane during the 1938 Empire Air Day at Hornchurch on 28th May. A record-breaking 7,967 adults and 3,263 children attended the event. *(Author)*

Bottom: A visiting Handley Page Harrow I, pictured during the Empire Air Display with small private aircraft parked around it. *(Author)*

Top: An Avro Anson arrives during an open day at the aerodrome. *(RAF Hornchurch Association)*

Bottom: Gloster Gladiator K8013 of 65 Squadron is towed out of the hangar and prepared for flying. *(P. Morfill)*

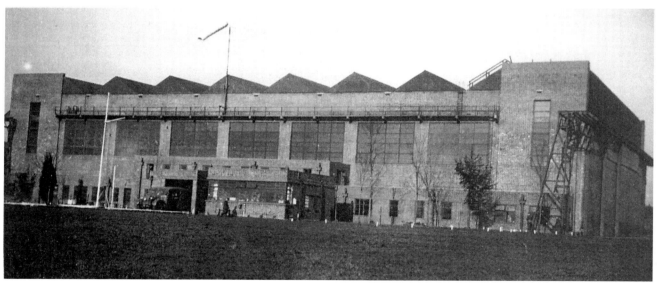

Top: An aerial view taken of RAF Hornchurch during 1938, showing the layout of the aerodrome. *(RAF Hornchurch Association)*

Bottom: An excellent view of the main C-type hangar at Hornchurch in 1938, with the Watch Office building just in front. *(A.C. Deere)*

Top: 5th August 1938. Hornchurch holds another Home Defence Exercise due to the ever-increasing international crisis in Europe with Hitler's Germany. Ground crew are seen wearing gasmasks during the exercise, but how can the man with the mobile telephone talk? A Gladiator aircraft of 65 Squadron is made ready behind. *(Author)*

Bottom: The remains of Flying Officer Gerald Saunders' Gladiator biplane after he misjudged his landing approach during a night flight on 10th October 1938. His aircraft's undercarriage hit one of the barn roofs of Albyn's Farm causing the aircraft to plough across a field before stopping short of the brick wall of one of the farm's outbuildings. Saunders climbed out from the aircraft unhurt, but sprained an ankle whilst tripping over some bricks near the wall. *(G. Saunders)*

Top: The barn roof, which was hit by Gerald Saunders' aircraft as he tried to land. *(G. Saunders)*

Bottom: A rare sight at Hornchurch. A Mark 1 two-bladed Hawker Hurricane fighter taken in early 1939. Next to the Hurricane can be seen a Miles Magister trainer. *(P. Morfill)*

This page: Two wonderful aerial photographs showing an early Spitfire Mk1 of 65 Squadron high above the clouds.
The aircraft was being flown by Sgt Morfill, the photographs being taken by fellow squadron pilot, Sgt Stanley Hayes.
(Sgt P.S. Hayes)

Top: This one's for the scrap yard lads! Ground crew take apart this Spitfire after it crashed on landing following a training flight in early 1939. *(P. Morfill)*

Bottom: A Fairey Battle monoplane at Hornchurch in early 1939. This aircraft was used by pilots for training, before they were converted to Spitfires. *(P. Morfill)*

Top: A Mk1 Spitfire of 74 Squadron wearing the pre-war codes of JH. Sporting white flying overalls are Flying Officer 'Sammy' Hoare and Pilot Officer Browne. *(D.S. Hoare)*

Bottom: Sergeant Philip Tew with his Spitfire, wearing his Irvin leather flying jacket. Note the thin radio mast that was in use at this time; these were modified by the start of war. *(Author)*

This page: A Spitfire is unceremoniously towed off the main grass flightpath by lorry, and pushed by a team of ground personnel back towards the main hangar, after suffering mechanical failure. *(Sgt P.S. Hayes)*

Top left: Sergeant Pilot Patrick Stanley Hayes in his Spitfire cockpit. Hayes was with 65 Squadron and was also a keen amateur photographer. A selection of some of the photographs he took at Hornchurch have been included within this book. Sadly he was listed as missing in action over the Channel on 7th July 1940, when Messerschmitt Bf109s bounced him and two others from the squadron. *(Sgt P.S. Hayes)*

Top right: Pilots of 65 and 74★ Squadron at the time of the last Empire Air Display in May 1939. Left to right: Sgt P.F. Morfill, Sgt Bushell★, Sgt N.T. Phillips, Sgt P.H. Tew, Sgt W.H. Franklin. *(Sgt P.S. Hayes)*

Bottom: A Spitfire of 65 Squadron is about to be towed back into the hangar by a mobile crane vehicle, for repair after it nosed over on landing. Note the bent propeller blades. *(Sgt P.S. Hayes)*

Let's get a closer look. Some 250 cadets of the Officers Training Corps Air Section arrived at Hornchurch on 1st August 1939. They were taken around various parts of the station and showed keen interest when given the chance to view the Spitfires. James Leathart of 54 Squadron is walking away on left of picture. Also note the Bristol Blenheim aircraft further along the aircraft line-up. The Spitfires coded DL, are of 54 Squadron before they changed to their wartime code of KL. (*Keystone*)

54

CHAPTER 3

IT'S WAR!

1939-1940

At 11.15 am on Sunday 3rd September 1939, Prime Minster Neville Chamberlain delivered his speech by radio to the British nation, telling them that for the second time in just over 20 years, they would now be at war with Germany.

At Hornchurch the pilots of 54, 65 and 74 Squadrons gathered around the radio and listened and wondered what now lay ahead. The previous months had seen them practicing fighter command tactics, but would they be a match for the tried and tested Luftwaffe, which had gained first hand combat experience in the recent Spanish Civil War?

Strangely, although war had been declared the aerodrome played host during those first few days to a film camera team from London Films, who were shooting flying sequences for a semi-documentary about Fighter and Bomber Command titled 'The Lion has Wings.' The flying sequences were carried out by B Flight, 74 Squadron and various still photographs were also taken, some of which are included in this book.

On 6th September the first alarm bells were sounded when an unidentified aircraft was picked up by radar coming in over the Essex coast. RAF fighters from nearby North Weald aerodrome were scrambled, as were Spitfires of 74 Squadron. Unfortunately fate and bad radar communication played its hand that day, when the Hurricane aircraft from North Weald were mistaken by pilots from Hornchurch as the enemy and subsequently two Hurricanes were shot down, one of the pilots being killed. This friendly fire incident was later known in RAF circles as the 'Battle of Barking Creek.'

After the first few dramatic days of war, things began to settle down into a period of mundane inactivity, waiting for the Germans' next move. Patrols were sent up to investigate the many unidentified plots during September and October, but no enemy contact or combat was met. The following months of late 1939 and early 1940 would become known as the 'Phoney War'.

During that October, the aerodrome received another band of men. 600 'City of London', who arrived led by their squadron commander, Squadron Leader The Viscount

Carlow. The squadron was equipped with the Bristol Blenheim Mk1F light-bombers and later operated from one of Hornchurch's forward airfields, RAF Manston. On 20th November, the aerodrome achieved its first score of the war, when 74 Squadron recorded a Heinkel bomber destroyed over the Thames estuary, near Southend. One month later, in December, a new station commander was appointed when Group Captain C.H. Nicholas was replaced by Group Captain Cecil Bouchier.

Bouchier had previously commanded 54 Squadron in 1936/37 and knew many of the pilots who still remained and he was well respected. He was delighted with his new appointment and he set out to make Hornchurch aerodrome the most prestigious and smartest in Fighter Command. The roads and paths were cleared up and paving stone edges were whitewashed. Grass verges and lawns were cut and great numbers of bulbs, plants and rose trees were planted. Every squadron was given tools to cultivate its own part of the camp.

Finally after months of planning, the Germans began their offensive operation on 10th May 1940, when Hitler ordered his Panzer divisions across the borders of Belgium and Holland. On 15th, a second attack was made through the Ardennes in a move to outflank the defensive fortress of the French Maginot Line, which ran from Luxembourg to Switzerland. As the lightning thrust of the German Panzers and the Luftwaffe began to take effect, the Allied armies were pushed back in disarray, totally outfought and out manoeuvred by the new German tactics of Blitzkrieg.

As the situation worsened on the continent,

the first patrols by squadrons based at Hornchurch were sent to fly over the Belgian coast on 16th May. 65 Squadron claimed a Junkers Ju88 shot down near Flushing the following day by Flying Officer J.H. Welford at 8 am.

By 20th May, the situation in France and Belgium had become so bad that plans for the evacuation of the British Expeditionary Force had been put forward under the supervision of Vice-Admiral Bertram Ramsey. The evacuation would take place around the port of Dunkirk and the codename for the operation would be 'Dynamo'.

Hornchurch squadrons would now be in the forefront of the action, with the task of patrolling and maintaining air cover over the port and beaches, while the ships and boats came in to pick up the army now under constant attack from Luftwaffe bombers.

Day after day, Spitfires from Hornchurch crossed the Channel to intercept and do battle with the Luftwaffe, who were causing carnage on the beaches below. The Hornchurch squadrons were further complemented during the operation, when 19 Squadron flew down from Duxford, 41 Squadron came south from Catterick in North Yorkshire and 222 Natal Squadron arrived from Kirton-in-Lindsey, Lincolnshire. During this period, it is recorded that Pilot Officer Alan Deere claimed the first combat encounter and victory against a Messerschmitt Bf 109 fighter, and that Flight Lieutenant James Leathart showed extreme bravery in the rescue attempt of a fellow squadron leader who had force-landed his Spitfire at Calais-Marck aerodrome, after his aircraft had suffered damage from combat. Leathart in a two-seat Miles Master trainer had flown back across to France under escort with two of his 54 Squadron comrades and rescued Squadron Leader White of 74 Squadron under the guns of advancing enemy tanks. Both these events took place on 23rd May 1940.

The operation to evacuate troops from Dunkirk continued until 4th June. Over 338,000 Allied troops had been successfully brought off the beaches and taken back to England. For Hornchurch's part it had lost 23 pilots killed or captured, but the sacrifice had not been in vain. The role played by the RAF during the Dunkirk evacuation has often been overlooked. Many soldiers said that they never saw the RAF while on the beaches and that it had been of little use. The truth is that most of the interceptions by the RAF against the Luftwaffe were high above the smoke and clouds of burning oil tanks at Dunkirk or above cloud base or just inland of the beaches. The fact is that the casualties of troops on the beaches would have been considerably higher, if the pilots of Fighter Command had not been actively engaging and shooting down German bombers and fighters.

On 10th June, Italy declared war against Britain, while on 18th June, Britain's Prime Minister, Winston Churchill declared in a speech in the House of Commons, that the Battle of France was over. The Battle of Britain was about to begin.

At Hornchurch, new replacement pilots and aircraft were posted in to make up for the casualties suffered over Dunkirk. They now waited for Hitler's next move.

Fortunately for Britain and Fighter Command, he and his commanders did not move against this country immediately. This gave Fighter Command the time and breathing space to replenish aircraft and train new pilots for the battle that lay ahead.

54 Squadron was sent to Hornchurch's forward airfield at Rochford, near Southend

on 25th May and while there received a signal from Hornchurch on 27th, that three of its officers, Alan Deere, Johnny Allen and James Leathart were to return immediately as a VIP would be visiting the aerodrome that morning and they would be introduced to him. The VIP in question was his Majesty King George VI, who was visiting Hornchurch to present medals to the pilots as a reward for their shooting down of enemy aircraft and their bravery in action. Those awarded honours that day were: Flight Lieutenant 'Sailor' Malan, Flight Lieutenant Robert Stanford Tuck, Pilot Officer John Allen and Flight Lieutenant Alan Deere. They each received the Distinguished Flying Cross, while Squadron Leader James Leathart was awarded the Distinguished Service Order for his action during the Calais-Marck rescue.

During the early part of July 1940, the squadrons were mainly employed in the protection of convoy shipping in the Channel areas and it was here that the next aerial operations against Britain began. This was the beginning of what would later be known as the first phase of the Battle of Britain, although the official records state the Battle started on 10th July. The Luftwaffe sent their bombers including the dreaded Stuka dive-bombers against the helpless British merchantmen, who could only try to avoid the falling bombs by zig-zagging their vessels in the hope of not being hit. The first skirmishes with squadrons at Hornchurch and other Fighter Command airfields began in earnest on 6th July with heavy fighting between the RAF and the German escort fighters, who were protecting the bombers. On one patrol, on 7th July 65 Squadron lost three of their pilots, when unseen enemy fighters bounced them. One of the pilots lost was Sergeant Patrick Stanley Hayes, who had joined 65 Squadron before the war.

The fighting continued, but changeable weather brought some days of respite for Fighter Command. 54 Squadron was ordered to Catterick for a rest period on 25th July, its replacement being 41 Squadron. At the beginning of August other pilots arrived at the aerodrome to replenish the casualties that were now beginning to mount. One new arrival who would soon be noticed for his skill in air-fighting, was a young Irishman from Dublin, Brendan 'Paddy' Finucane, who joined 65 Squadron.

On 13th August 1940, the Germans launched *Adler Tag* or Eagle Day, the second phase of the battle, which was to launch attacks against RAF airfields and installations. The raids using massed bomber formations with fighter escort were intended to destroy many of the RAF fighters on the ground as well as in the air and render the aerodromes inoperative. Fortunately Hornchurch was not attacked, but forward airfields like Manston received a heavy pasting and suffered substantial damage to its hangars and buildings.

The enemy raids continued until 19th August, and the squadrons were put under a great strain. Fortunately the weather deteriorated on that day with cloudy skies and rain limiting the number of German operations over the Channel; the bad weather lasted until 23rd August. This short lull in the fighting gave the Hornchurch squadrons time to rest and unwind, while the ground crew and station personnel could re-equip and repair damaged aircraft. A more serious problem was the replacement rate of new pilots. The squadrons were receiving new inexperienced pilots with only a few hours on Spitfires, and many had not even fired their guns in anger.

On 22nd August another squadron flew in from Kirton-in-Lindsey; not another Spitfire squadron, but 264 'Madras' Squadron operating the Boulton Paul Defiant. The Defiant was a monoplane fighter developed on the same lines as the old two-seat Bristol Fighter of the First World War, with a pilot and a gunner. The gunner was seated in a separate turret behind the pilot, and he had the firepower of four .303 Browning machine guns. Unfortunately the designers had not deemed it necessary to fit forward-firing machine guns in the wings of the aircraft.

The Defiant had performed well and had claimed many victories during the Dunkirk operations against bombers and some German fighters, but the Germans now knew of its weakness of frontal attacks from below. The pilots and gunners of 264 Squadron were nevertheless undaunted by the task they had been given as they arrived at Hornchurch.

The weather returned to perfect flying conditions for 24th August and the Luftwaffe resumed its operations. At 12.30 pm, Defiant aircraft who had flown down to operate from Manston earlier that morning, took off from the aerodrome and intercepted a number of Junker Ju88s, but were caught by enemy fighters who shot down three of the squadron including their commanding officer Squadron Leader Philip Hunter who was listed as missing. The survivors returned to Hornchurch, but they were caught on the ground as the first enemy raid on Hornchurch was sounded. One Defiant was lost, when Messerschmitts of JG51 shot it down close to the aerodrome.

Hornchurch was again targeted on the 26th, together with the aerodromes at Kenley, Biggin Hill, North Weald and Debden. On 28th August, a fresh new squadron arrived from Turnhouse in Scotland – 603 'City of Edinburgh' Squadron. The next day on 29th

August, after spending six years as one of Hornchurch's home-based squadrons, 65 Squadron was posted to Turnhouse never to return again. The Defiants of 264 Squadron were also withdrawn from the day battle at this stage and their place was taken by 222 Squadron down from Kirton-in-Lindsey.

The following two days saw increased raids and the aerodrome was attacked twice on 31st August, causing damage mainly to the flightpath; the aerodrome continued to remain operational, although some of the squadrons were diverted to other airfields, until bomb craters had been filled in and unexploded bombs made safe.

On 3rd September another of the long-standing serving squadrons bade farewell to Hornchurch for the final time, when 54 was sent to Catterick for rest, 41 Squadron taking its place.

Throughout the rest of September 41, 222 and 603 Squadrons battled with the Luftwaffe, mainly dealing with the high escort German fighters. On 15th September, the Germans who thought that Fighter Command was down to its last few aircraft, were shocked into reality, when they were not only confronted by the squadrons from 11 Group, but a wing of 60 fighter aircraft from 12 Group as well. The Luftwaffe suffered the loss of 56 aircraft that day and arrived back at their bases in France knowing that the RAF was far from beaten. In October, the German tactics of heavy massed bomber formations had given way to fighter-bomber sweeps, which had no tactical significance on the outcome of the battle.

When the Battle of Britain ended, Hornchurch could lay claim to having had the top-scoring squadron with 603 Squadron claiming 58 enemy aircraft destroyed and the top-scoring pilot, with 41 Squadron's Eric Lock destroying 20 enemy aircraft and 7

probably destroyed. It also should be remembered however that 68 of Hornchurch's pilots and aircrew were killed in action securing Britain from the threat of invasion at this most crucial period of the war.

During November and December 1940, two new squadrons flew in to operate from the aerodrome; these were 64 and 611 Squadrons, who replaced 222 and 603, while 41 remained to continue operations. On 24th December, a new station commander was appointed to replace Group Captain Bouchier who was now appointed to a new role at 11 Group Headquarters. His position was taken by Wing Commander Harry Broadhurst, who would lead the Hornchurch squadrons in the new offensive operations planned for 1941.

Top: Hornchurch aerodrome 3rd September 1939, the day war was declared. Bell tents are erected out on dispersal around the east edge of the flightpath and the pilots await Germany's next move. *(P. Morfill)*

Bottom: Pilots of B Flight 74 Squadron take a short break between filling sandbags to construct temporary blast pens for their aircraft at dispersal. Left to right are: F/O Hoare, F/O Thom, F/Lt Treacy, P/O Browne and F/O Manwaring. *(D.S. Hoare)*

Top: Time you had a haircut young sir! Robert Stanford Tuck (right) gives Hope-Boyd a quick snip as George Proudman (left) and Jack Kennedy check he's doing it properly, out at 65 Squadron's dispersal during the early part of September after war had been declared. *(Sgt P.S. Hayes)*

Bottom: A Spitfire of 54 Squadron stands ready for take-off with the electric trolley starter (on right) plugged in ready to start up the machine. This aircraft was flown by F/O Basil 'Wonky' Way. Way was killed in action on 25th July 1940 after having shot down an Me109. He crashed into the Channel, his body was washed ashore sometime later and he was buried in the Ostdunkerke Communal Cemetery, Belgium. *(C. Gray)*

Top: Pilots of 54 Squadron out at dispersal await orders during the first few hours of war. P/O Johnny Allen is pictured left, then Sgt Jack Davis and F/O George Gribble centre with tunic on, others unknown. *(A.C Deere)*

Bottom: A front-on view of a Mk1a Spitfire of 74 Squadron with its undersides painted black and white. This scheme was used early on during the war as identification for the ground defences to distinguish between friend and foe. *(D.S. Hoare)*

Top: The chaps in A Flight. Waiting for their first action, pilots of 54 Squadron pose for a group photograph. Left to right: F/Lt Max Pearson, Sgt Jack Davis, P/O George Coussens, F/Lt James Leathart, F/O George Gribble, P/O Johnny Allen and P/O Alan Deere. *(A.C. Deere)*

Bottom: Pilot Officer Alan Deere's Spitfire KL-B parked in the newly prepared and sandbagged dispersal pen. Deere, a New Zealander, would become a leading ace and commander during the war. *(A.C. Deere)*

Top: Ready to start up! Aircraft of 65 Squadron prepare to take to the air. The ground crew standby to start the Spitfire's engine with the electrical starter trolley. (Sgt *P.S. Hayes*)

Bottom: Sgt Pilot Percy Morfill of 65 Squadron relaxing inside one of the squadron's bell tents, situated out at dispersal. (Sgt *P.S. Hayes*)

Top: Ready for Jerry? One of Hornchurch's machine-gun pits, set up around the airfield for defence at the outbreak of war. The gunner is operating a Lewis machine gun, first developed during WW1. *(Sgt P.S. Hayes)*

Bottom: An aircraft of 65 Squadron stands ready to take off. Note that the squadron code letters have now changed from pre-war FZ to YT. This was done hopefully to confuse the Germans. *(Sgt P.S. Hayes)*

Ironically, it was during the first few days of war that a film crew from The London Film Company descended upon Hornchurch to shoot footage of the Spitfires for a forthcoming film titled 'The Lion has Wings'. The squadron chosen to supply the flying sequences was 74 Squadron, with mainly pilots from B Flight. The film was directed by Alexander Korda and starred Ralph Richardson and Merle Oberon. The following three photographs were taken at the time.

Top: The camera crew prepare to start filming at 74 Squadron's dispersal. *(D.S. Hoare)*

Bottom: Three of 74's pilots take a break during the filming sequences: Left to right: F/Lt 'Paddy' Treacy, F/O 'Sammy' Hoare and F/Sgt Ernie Mayne. *(D.S. Hoare)*

Top: B Flight of 74 Squadron pose for a casual photograph:
Left to right: F/O G.A.P. Manwaring, F/O D. Thom,
P/O D.H.T. Dowding, F/Lt W.P. Treacy (standing),
F/O D.S. Hoare, F/Sgt E. Mayne and Sgt Bushell. Pilot Officer
Dowding was son of Air Chief Marshal Sir Hugh Dowding,
Commander–in–Chief of Fighter Command. *(D.S. Hoare)*

Bottom: A Bristol Blenheim of 600
Squadron comes to grief on landing at
Hornchurch, when its undercarriage
collapses, during the winter of 1939/40.
(IWM MH 8289)

Top: A view of the firing butts at Hornchurch. A Spitfire of 54 Squadron has been raised level with the aid of a hydraulic trestle and is now ready to have its guns harmonized and tested. *(D.S. Hoare)*

Bottom: King George VI visited RAF Hornchurch on 27th June 1940, to bestow gallantry awards to five officers. This photograph shows Squadron Leader James Anthony Leathart being awarded his Distinguished Service Order for his courage during the Dunkirk evacuation. Leathart had flown a Miles Master training aircraft to Calais–Marck aerodrome to rescue a fellow squadron commander, who had been shot down there, but was uninjured. Whilst taking off, after the rescue, enemy fighters attacked Leathart's aircraft and he was forced to make an emergency landing and vacate the aircraft to take cover in a nearby slit trench. After a few minutes the enemy disappeared. Leathart and the rescued pilot managed to start up the Miles Master and take off and return across the Channel to safety. *(IWM CH 443)*

'Well Done Johnny'. King George VI congratulates Pilot Officer Johnny Allen of 54 Squadron after presenting him with the Distinguished Flying Cross. Allen received the award for his actions over Dunkirk and Calais-Marck in May 1940. To the King's left is Air Chief Marshal Sir Hugh Dowding, Commander-in Chief of Fighter Command. Allen was killed only a few weeks later in combat against Messerschmitt 109s over Margate on 23rd July. *(A.C. Deere)*

Top: Three cheers for His Majesty the King! The six Hornchurch aces raise their caps after receiving their awards. Left to right: P/O John Allen DFC, 54 Sqdn, F/Lt Robert Stanford Tuck, DFC, 92 Sqdn, F/Lt Alan Deere, DFC, 54 Sqdn, F/Lt Adolph Malan, DFC, 74 Sqdn, S/Ldr James Leathart, DSO, 54 Sqdn and unnamed bugler. *(A.C. Deere)*

Bottom: The 17 pilots and two ground officers of 54 Squadron, taken just before the opening of the Battle of Britain. Of the pilots only nine survived the war. Left to right: Back row, Sgt W. Lawrence, Sgt G. Collett★, ground officer, P/O D. McMullen, P/O P. Howes★, P/O A. Finnie★, P/O D. Turley-George, P/O H. Matthews★, F/Sgt Tew, P/O C. Gray, Middle row: P/O J. Allen★, F/Lt A. Deere, S/Ldr J. Leathart, F/Lt B. Way★, P/O G. Gribble★. Front row: Sgt J. Norwell, P/O E. Coleman★, P. Shallard (intelligence officer), P/O W. Hopkins. (★Killed during the war) *(A.C. Deere)*

Top: VIP visits 65 Squadron. Captain Balfour, the Under Secretary of State for Air, visited Hornchurch on 15th July 1940, when 65 Squadron was presented with eight new aircraft from monies raised from the East India Company Fund. In front of one of the new Spitfires are from left to right: Sgt MacPherson, F/O Nicholas, P/O Grant, F/O Olive, Capt Balfour, S/Ldr Sawyer, F/Lt Saunders, F/O Smart and P/O Kilner. *(G. Saunders)*

Bottom: Flying Officer Smart in the cockpit of one of the new Spitfires paid for by the East India Company. *(G. Saunders)*

Top: 'Sailor' Malan of 74 Squadron would become one of the great aces and fighter leaders of the war. Here he is with his Spitfire ZP-A down at Manston. *(D.S. Hoare)*

Bottom: Pilots of 54 Squadron at their wooden dispersal hut, find time to have this photograph taken as they await their next sortie. Note the large Air Ministry bell, which was rung when the squadron was ordered to scramble. Left to right: Sgt Joseph Lockwood, F/O George Gribble, ?, and F/O Desmond McMullen. August 1940. *(Author)*

Near Bradwell Bank

Let a single Me. 109 – a "filter" go rather than loose height.

Top: Pilot Officer Harbourne Mackay Stephen of 74 'Tiger' Squadron stands on the main-plane of his Spitfire down at Hornchurch's most forward airfield at Manston in July 1940. This photo has been stuck in his logbook. (H.M. Stephen)

Bottom: Three Supermarine Spitfire Mk 1As (including R6712 YT-N and R6714 YT-M of 65 Squadron) take off from Hornchurch on 13th August 1940. (IWM HU 54421)

Top: A Spitfire of 74 Squadron under repair in a hangar at Hornchurch during the Battle of Britain. The gentleman pictured on the left is Warrant Officer Ernest 'Tubby' Mayne, who was the oldest pilot to participate in the battle, aged 39 years. *(Author)*

Bottom: Pilots of 65 Squadron relax between sorties, based at Hornchurch's satellite airfield at Rochford. Left to right: S/Ldr Holland, F/Lt Saunders in front, Intelligence Officer Hardy, F/Lt Olive, F/O Wigg, P/O Hart and P/O Glaser. *(D. Glaser)*

Top left: Flying Officer John Mungo-Park of 74 Squadron, who became an ace with 11 confirmed victories, before he was lost over the Channel on 27th June 1941. *(H.M. Stephen)*

Top right: Replacement pilots were urgently needed during the Battle of Britain, when Fighter Command's losses began to rise in August 1940. One such pilot was young Les Harvey who as a Sgt Pilot joined 54 Squadron in mid August with only 4 hours and 20 minutes experience on Spitfires. Les survived the battle and the war. *(L. Harvey)*

Bottom: One of the few Polish pilots who flew from Hornchurch during the Battle of Britain was Boleslaw Drobinski. After arriving in England in January 1940, he was sent to RAF Eastchurch for an induction course and tuition in English. He then spent some time with No.2 School of Army Co-operation at Old Sarum, before converting to Spitfires at 7 Operational Training Unit at Hawarden. He arrived at Hornchurch on 12th August 1940. He survived the war and died in August 1995. *(D. Glaser)*

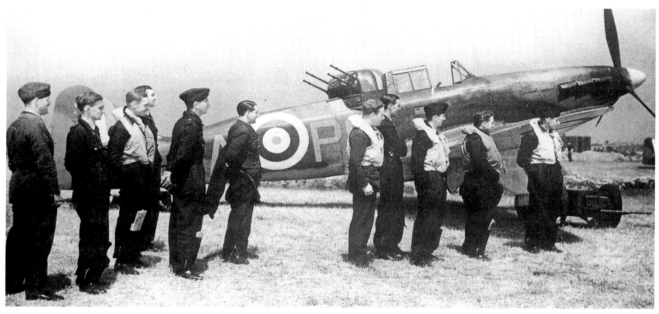

Top: Aircrew of 264 Squadron, who flew the Defiant aircraft, on their way to dispersal. Many of these men were to be killed whilst flying from Hornchurch and Manston during August, when the German fighters literally knocked them out of the sky. Ten of the squadron's aircraft were destroyed between 24th and 28th August. Those recognised in the photograph on the back of the lorry are left to right: 1st standing S/Ldr Philip Hunter★, 2nd standing LAC Fred King★, 3rd seated P/O C.E. Johnson★, 5th standing LAC Fred Barker and 8th standing LAC Robert Turner★. In the lorry is Sgt A.R. Launder. (★ Killed in action) *(IWM CH 193)*

Bottom: 264 Squadron await the order to take to the air. The Boulton Paul Defiant with its Frazer Nash turret of four x 0.303 Browning machine guns was lethal, but the aircraft lacked forward armament and soon suffered high casualties and was withdrawn from the battle. Left to right are: 2nd P/O D.S Kay, P/O G. Hackwood, P/O D. Whitely,?, S/Ldr P. Hunter, P/O S. Thomas, F/Lt N. Cooke, P/O M. Young, P/O H. Goodhall and P/O Barwell. *(IWM CH 195)*

Top: 222 Natal Squadron were posted down to Hornchurch at the end of August 1940 from Kirton-in-Lindsey, Lincolnshire. Most of the squadron's ground crew travelled down by RAF transport, but airframe rigger Joe Crawshaw drove down in his own Austin 7 car, registration HX8739, which he bought for £10.00 at Kirton and sprayed in camouflage colours. The photograph shows Joe in his car at Hornchurch on 4th September 1940. *(J. Crawshaw)*

Bottom: A mechanic and rigger of 222 Natal Squadron stand proudly by their aircraft in late August 1940. *(IWM HU 44700)*

This page and top opposite: Three photographs showing the bombing of Hornchurch on 31st August 1940. The gentleman who took these photographs must have had nerves of steel. *(A.C. Deere)*

This page, bottom: The aftermath of a German raid on the aerodrome on 31st August. A Spitfire lies wrecked beyond repair. *(J. Crawshaw)*

Top: The flower of Britain's youth! Four Sergeant Pilots of 222 Natal Squadron: Left to right: Sidney Baxter, John Ramshaw, Leon Patrick and Douglas Chipping. John Ramshaw died on 4th September 1940, after being shot down by enemy fighters and crash-landing his aircraft at Marden in Kent. He suffered severe head injuries and died before reaching hospital. Sid Baxter was killed on 14th September, when his aircraft spun into the ground, just short of the airfield. His Spitfire's tail-section broke away from the main fuselage, due to damage suffered in combat. Both Chipping and Patrick survived the war. *(J. Berryman)*

Bottom: Spitfires of 222 Squadron are prepared for the next sortie by ground crew out at dispersal at the south-east end of the aerodrome at the start of September. Spitfire ZD-D X4278 was shot down on 4th September over Maidstone, its pilot Flying Officer John Cutts being killed. Spitfire XT-M X4277 belonged to 603 Squadron and was shot down over Margate on 3rd September. The pilot, Flying Officer Richard Hillary baled out into the sea and was rescued by the Margate lifeboat, the *J.B. Proudfoot*, suffering from burns and shock. *(J. Crawshaw)*

Top: Returning from combat on 1st September, a Spitfire is stranded in the middle of the flightpath, having run out of fuel. This photograph was taken by Joe Crawshaw, a rigger with 222 Squadron. Immediately afterwards, he and another crewman grabbed a vehicle and towed the aircraft to the dispersal area. In the background between the two Spitfires can be seen a Boulton Paul Defiant of 264 Squadron and in the E-pens to the right are three Bristol Blenheims of 600 Squadron. *(J. Crawshaw)*

Bottom: The dashing young fighter pilot! Pilot Officer Richard Hope Hillary, who flew with 603 City of Edinburgh Squadron. He achieved ace status quickly before being shot down over Margate on 3rd September 1940. He managed to bale out of his stricken aircraft, but suffered terrible burns to his face and hands. *(D. Ross Collection)*

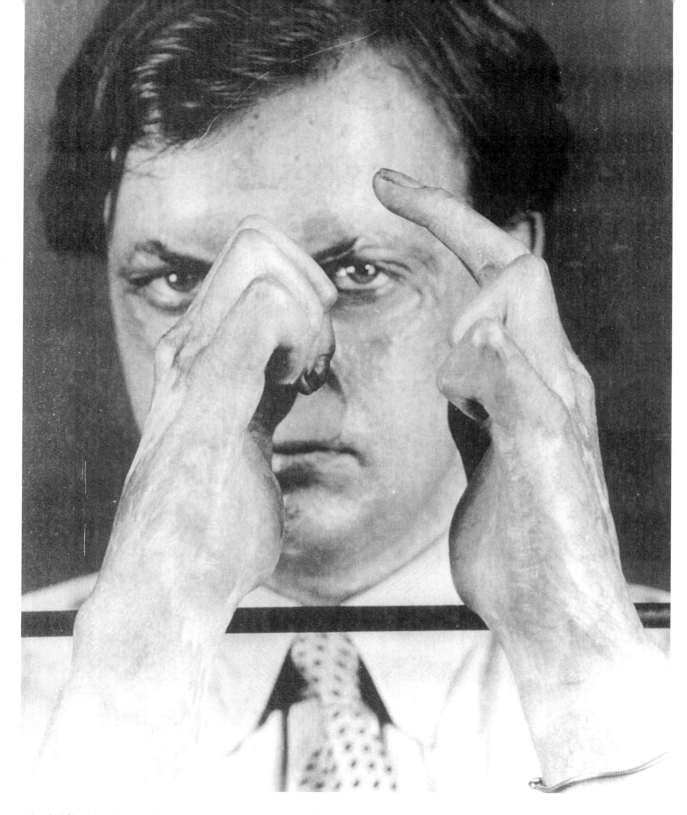

The half hidden burnt face and hands of Richard Hillary after he had undergone constructive surgery by the pioneering plastic surgeon Sir Archibald McIndoe. *(D. Ross Collection)*

Top: Sergeant Pilot John Burgess of 222, in his flying kit at Hornchurch's forward satellite base at Rochford. *(J. Burgess)*

Bottom: Spitfire Mk1As being serviced, while in the background two aircraft take off during the Battle of Britain in September 1940. *(IWM HU 54411)*

Previous page, top: 222 Natal Squadron ground crew at Hornchurch. From left to right back row: Bill Dashper, Dave Davis, Anderson, Lance Lidgett, Nobby Clarke. On wing: first two unknown, Chalky White and Monty in cockpit. *(Joe Crawshaw)*

This page, top: Pilot Officer Ronald 'Ras' Berry of 603 'City of Edinburgh' Squadron with his aircraft. The officer standing to the right is the squadron's intelligence officer, Pilot Officer W. L. Blackbourn. *(R. Berry)*

Bottom: Spitfires of 222 Natal Squadron climb through the early morning mist on another patrol during September 1940. The infamous laundry chimney of St George's Hospital can be clearly seen. *(J. Crawshaw)*

Top: Desperately tired, but still fighting. A weary looking Pilot Officer Philip 'Pip' Cardell of 603 Squadron poses with his aircraft XT-V – P9553 at dispersal. A few days after this photo was taken, Cardell was killed over the Channel, when the Spitfire he was flying, N3244, was attacked by enemy fighters. He had been wounded during the engagement and was trying to make landfall, but was forced to bale out near the coast at Folkestone and went into the water, his parachute failing to deploy. A fellow pilot, Pilot Officer Peter Dexter tried to attract the attention of people on the beach to the incident, but this was to no avail. Dexter bravely landed his aircraft on the beach and commandeered a small boat to rescue Cardell. Sadly on reaching him they found he was already dead. He was 23 years old. *(D. Ross Collection)*

Bottom: Spitfires of 222 Squadron get quickly airborne after being scrambled as another Luftwaffe raid is picked up by radar crossing the Channel. *(RAF Museum)*

Top: Men of the Royal Artillery are pictured in front of their 4.5 inch anti-aircraft gun. These men together with 109th Canadian Light Anti-Aircraft Battery, which operated eight Bofor guns, were given the task of protecting the airfield, if it should come under aerial attack. *(Author)*

Bottom: Spitfire P9512 lies smashed after its pilot Sgt John McAdam of 41 Squadron was forced to undertake an emergency landing, when the aircraft's engine cut out just after take-off at 4.40 pm on 12th October 1940. McAdam crash-landed at Globe Road, Hornchurch and was himself miraculously unhurt. *(John Hewitt)*

Top: The tail-wheel from Spitfire P9512 was taken by a local resident as a souvenir at the time. It is now part of the RAF Hornchurch Association Collection. *(RAF Hornchurch Association)*

Bottom: Sgt Pilot Terry Healy seated on the nose of a 41 Squadron Spitfire smiles for the camera, totally unaware of the prankster with two fingers held high, October 1940. Healy was killed on 2nd March 1944 whilst serving with 266 Squadron, aged 23. *(R. Beardsley)*

Tail-wheel and fuel-line component Retrieved to me from the Globe Road crash

Top: Sgt Pilot John McAdam. He was killed in action on 20th February 1941, shot down during a patrol off Dover, when the squadron was bounced by enemy fighters. *(John Hewitt)*

Bottom: Engine mechanic Chalky White of 222 Squadron with his Spitfire in October 1940. *(Joe Crawshaw)*

Top: A view of the aircraft dispersal pens as Squadron Leader Donald Finlay of 41 Squadron strides across in front of the camera lens. October 1940. *(Frank Mileham)*

Bottom: Pilot Officer Denys Mileham seated on the wing of his Spitfire in October 1940. Mileham was posted to 41 Squadron on 29th September and claimed a Messerschmitt 109 destroyed on 5th October. He was killed in action on 15th April 1942, whilst serving with 234 Squadron. His body was never recovered and he is now remembered on the Runnymede Memorial, Panel 66. *(Frank Mileham)*

Top: Pilots of 41 Squadron line up for the press at Hornchurch in November 1940. Left to right: New Zealander Flying Officer John Mackenzie, Flight Lieutenant Tony Lovell, Squadron Leader Donald Finlay, Flight Lieutenant Norman Ryder and Pilot Officer Roy Ford.
(R. Beardsley)

Bottom: Cut the cake Norman! Pilots of 41 Squadron look on as F/Lt Norman Ryder cuts his birthday cake on 28th November 1940. Left to right: S/Ldr Don Finlay, F/O Dennis Adams, Sgt John Angus, Sgt Terry Healy, Sgt John Gilders, F/Lt Ryder, P/O Norman McHardy-Brown and P/O Michael Briggs.
(IWM CH 1866)

CHAPTER 4

ON THE OFFENSIVE

1941

At the beginning of 1941, Hornchurch along with other fighter and bomber aerodromes received new orders and instructions from their head of commands with regard to offensive operations, to take the fight to the Germans back across the Channel. Hornchurch would be involved in the new fighter sweep missions named Circus, Rodeo, Rhubarb and Ramrod. The first operation in which Hornchurch squadrons would partake was on 10th January 1941. The mission was to bomb the Forêt de Guines airfield in north-west France. Hornchurch would provide fighter escort to six Bristol Blenheim bombers with 41, 64 and 611 Squadrons. The operation was successful and no bombers were lost on the raid. During this time all the squadrons were flying the Spitfire MkIIb aircraft.

In February 41 Squadron left Hornchurch for the last time and exchanged places with 54 Squadron stationed at Catterick. With the ever-increasing sweeps over northern France, the British bombers would be escorted by larger formations of fighter aircraft known as wings, so was born the Hornchurch Wing,

along with similar wings from other aerodromes, Kenley, Biggin Hill, North Weald and so on.

Another change of squadrons took place on 16th May when 64 Squadron left to be replaced by 603 Squadron who had been based there the previous year and had done such sterling work.

By June 1941, the Hornchurch squadrons had converted to the new variant MkV Spitfire. The aircraft had been fitted with a Rolls-Royce Merlin 45 engine that gave better performance in altitude and ceiling height. The improved armament of two 20-millimetre Hispano cannons and four .303 machine guns instead of the previous eight, gave the aircraft more deadly and hard-hitting firepower. More importantly the aircraft's speed in flight at 20,000 feet was 371 mph. The MkV helped to neutralise the advantage that the Germans had at this stage, as they had improved their own fighter, the Messerschmitt 109E to the F design.

The armed escort of RAF bombers on raids continued throughout the following months and were at times costly in losses of experienced pilots and commanders. Hornchurch lost Wing Commander Joe Kayll on 25th June; fortunately he managed to crash land his aircraft, but was captured. At the beginning of August, the ace pilot Flight Lieutenant Eric Lock was lost during a sortie over Boulogne whilst attacking ground troops. On 3rd August the first Commonwealth squadron arrived at Hornchurch, when 403 'Wolf' Canadian Squadron flew in from Ternhill to replace 54 Squadron, but its stay would be brief and it had departed by the 25th that same month.

Command of the aerodrome was handed over to Wing Commander Frederick Stapleton, when Harry Broadhurst left to conduct a three-month Air Ministry goodwill trip to the United States in October.

A new RAF satellite airfield was officially opened at nearby Fairlop, near Barkingside, Essex on 12th November, with 603 Squadron operating from there immediately. On the same day, 611 Squadron left for Drem in Scotland. 54 Squadron, the longest serving squadron to be based at Hornchurch, left for the last time on 17th November, its place taken by 64. Another Canadian squadron, 411 'Grizzly Bear', flew in to start operations on the 22nd.

Group Captain Harry Broadhurst resumed his command, when he arrived back from America on 1st December, after touring the country giving lectures on fighter tactics. Six days later news of the entry of the United States into the war was heard over the aerodrome's Tannoy speaker system on 7th December, after Japan had attacked the American naval base at Pearl Harbor.

On 15th December, 603 Squadron left the Hornchurch Sector for the last time. The squadron had one of the most distinguished records of any unit that flew from the aerodrome. It would now continue that record with heroic actions in the defence of Malta. 603's place was taken by 313 Czechoslovakian Squadron, led by Squadron Leader Karal Mrazek. The Czechs had brought their own operations room controller with them in case their pilots had difficulty in language communication during operations over France.

As Christmas and New Year approached, the aerodrome was readied for festivities, with church services and entertainment laid on for pilots and ground personnel alike. 1941 had been an extremely demanding and busy year for all those involved at Hornchurch. They had taken the war back to the enemy and shown the Germans that Britain was far from beaten.

Top: In January 1941 Wing
Commander Harry
Broadhurst took over as the
new station commander.
Broadhurst is seen in this
photograph visiting a local
factory plant and being
presented with a model
Spitfire by the workers.
(H. Broadhurst)

Bottom: Sergeant Pilot Bob
Beardsley of 41 Squadron
in his Spitfire in early 1941.
(R. Beardsley)

Top: During a sweep over northern France on 26th February, Sergeant Pilot Howard Squire of 54 Squadron was shot down by Hauptmann Herbert Ihefeld, commander of Jagdgeschwader 77 over Calais. Squire was able to crash land his aircraft, but was almost immediately captured. The photograph shows Squire with his wrecked Spitfire surrounded by Luftwaffe officers including Ihefeld who is standing to the right of Squire. *(H. Squire)*

Bottom: After his capture, Howard Squire was taken to the German Officers' Mess at Calais-Marck airfield, where he was fed and given a glass of schnapps by the Luftwaffe airmen. Squire is in the ante-room of the Mess with his captors. *(H. Squire)*

Top: 54 Squadron pilots gather round for a press photo. Those identified are from 2nd left P/O A. Black, F/O J.S Harris, the squadron mascot, 'Crash' with S/Ldr Robert Finlay-Boyd, S/Ldr Jamie Rankin, of 64 Squadron, F/Lt H.N.D. Bailey, F/Lt Jack Charles, P/O Gordon Batchelor, F/Lt H.S. Sewell, P/O Powell & P/O A.R.M. Campbell. *(IWM CH 2710)*

Bottom: A Spitfire Vb of 611 'West Lancashire' Squadron swoops low over the airfield on its return from another sortie over northern France – June 1941. *(H. Broadhurst)*

This aerial photograph shows the airfield viewed looking north towards Hornchurch and Upminster in April 1941. The aerodrome still shows the scars from bombing in 1940 with filled-in crater holes still visible. (*Crown Copyright*)

Top: The pilots of 611 Squadron report to the intelligence officer on their return from operations to give him information on the day's combat. Left to right: Flying Officer Peter Dexter, Flight Lieutenant Clive Mellersh (IO), Sergeant Townsend, Flight Lieutenant Charlie Mears and Pilot Officer Wilfred Duncan Smith. *(IWM CH 3058)*

Bottom: Pilots of 54 Squadron discuss the sortie they have just returned from. Right to left: P/O Jack Charles, F/O Nigel Rose and P/O J.S 'Streak' Harris. *(H. Broadhurst)*

Top left: Flight Lieutenant Eric 'Sawn off' Lock gives the thumbs up, seated in his MkVb Spitfire. This picture was taken in late July 1941, when Lock had returned to operational flying with 611 Squadron. Lock had become a fighter ace during the Battle of Britain with 22 victories to his credit; later research showed he was the top scorer during the battle. Lock was listed as missing in action on 3rd August 1941, after failing to return from a sortie over Boulogne. *(IWM)*

Top centre: Sgt Pilot Harold Bennett served with 603 City of Edinburgh Squadron from 28th August until 8th December 1941. On that day, enemy fighters shot down Harold and two other squadron pilots during a raid over Hesdin, northern France. Fortunately Harold survived, but spent the remainder of the war as a prisoner. *(H. Bennett)*

Bottom: Pilots of 603 'City of Edinburgh' Squadron pictured with presentation Spitfire W3628, named 'Oman'. This aircraft was gifted to the squadron from the Persian Government and arrived from 6 Maintenance Unit on 24th July. The pilots are front row left to right: P/O Fawkes, Sgt Archibald and F/O H.G. Niven. On aircraft back row: Sgt Stone, P/O Keable, Sgt Ruchwaldy, F/O Griffiths, P/O Marland and F/Lt Scott–Malden. Seated on wing is P/O Falconer. *(D. Scott–Malden)*

Top: Safe return. A Spitfire Vb comes in to land over one of the many aircraft blast pens around the airfield. *(Author)*

Bottom: Canadian Squadron 411 'Grizzly Bear' lines up for a group photograph on a misty December day. Pictured 7th from left is American volunteer P/O William 'Tex' Ash, 9th is S/Ldr Stan Turner who previously had flown in 242 Squadron with Douglas Bader during 1940. *(W. Ash)*

CHAPTER 5

A MULTI-NATIONAL FIGHTING STATION

1942

At the very beginning of 1942, Hornchurch received a visit from the Commander-in-Chief of Fighter Command, Air Chief Marshal Sir William Sholto Douglas, who inspected the squadrons out at their dispersal areas. He praised them for the splendid work they had carried out the previous year and encouraged them to carry on their successes in the fight against the Hun.

On 12th February, Hornchurch squadrons were scrambled when news came through that the German battle cruisers *Scharnhorst* and *Gneisenau* together with the cruiser *Prinz Eugen* were trying to break out from the French port of Brest, back through the Channel to the German port of Wilhelmshaven.

The Hornchurch Wing consisting of 64 and 411 Squadrons had taken off from the satellite airfield at Fairlop with orders to rendezvous with Swordfish torpedo biplanes of 825 Squadron and escort them to the target. The Wing headed out along the coast, but failed to make contact with the Swordfish or even sight the enemy cruisers.

Despite this, 825 Squadron led by Lieutenant Commander Eugene Esmonde continued on its mission to attack the German ships, but in doing so was literally cut to pieces by the heavy German flak and Luftwaffe fighter defence that had been put up over the ships. Out of 18 aircrew, only three survived.

In March 411 Squadron moved out from the aerodrome and its place was taken by 122 'Bombay' Squadron led by Squadron Leader Frantisek Fajtl, a Czech who had flown during the Battle of Britain.

On 28th April, the aerodrome was visited by the President of the Czechoslovak national committee in exile, Mr Eduard Benes who together with his wife, presented medals to the pilots of 313 Czech Squadron.

A RAF film production unit under the guidance of the Ministry of Information arrived to film the squadrons of 64 and 122 on 7th May. General scenes of the squadrons at dispersal, taking off, landing and formation flying were filmed during their stay. On 15th May, Hornchurch received a new station commander, when Group Captain George

Lott DSO, DFC arrived from 13 Group to take over from Harry Broadhurst. 'Broady' had been promoted to Deputy Senior Air Staff Officer at 11 Group Headquarters.

On 21st June, the Hornchurch Wing received a new Wing Commander Flying - Squadron Leader Brendan 'Paddy' Finucane, who had flown with 65 Squadron at Hornchurch in 1940 and was now an ace with 26 enemy victories to his name. 'Paddy' was appointed to the acting rank of wing commander. Sadly his time at Hornchurch would only be brief, for on 15th July he was tragically lost on a sweep over France, when on the return leg of the mission, his aircraft was damaged by German ground fire and he was forced to ditch in the Channel. His Spitfire sank almost immediately carrying the unfortunate pilot to his death.

On 25th July, another new squadron arrived at the aerodrome for the first time. Led by its commanding officer Squadron Leader Bernard Duperier, 340 (Ile de France) Squadron came from Westhampnett in Sussex. The French pilots were thought to be very smart in their dark blue uniforms with gold braided cuffs. They brought with them their own ground crew, whose uniforms looked similar to those of French sailors.

The RAF's answer to the German Focke-Wulf 190 finally arrived after months of combat with the Luftwaffe on unequal terms that had seen Fighter Command struggling to keep pace with the enemy. 64 Squadron became the first to be equipped with the new Spitfire Mk IX and was declared operational at Hornchurch on the new type on 28th July 1942. Two days later, on the 30th, Flight Lieutenant Donald Kingaby claimed the first Focke-Wulf destroyed over Boulogne.

On 9th August, 64 Squadron carried out close practice formation with American B17 Flying Fortresses. Very soon the Hornchurch Wing would be asked to provide high escort cover for the daylight bombing raids operated by the Americans.

As dawn approached on 19th August 1942, pilots from many airfields in the south-east began to prepare themselves for Operation 'Jubilee', a large combined service raid against the harbour town of Dieppe. The operation consisted of landing over 6,000 British and Canadian troops to attack and destroy local defences and installations in and around the town, before withdrawal and pick-up by the navy. The RAF would provide air support and cover throughout the operation.

At Hornchurch, squadrons 64, 122 and 340 were ready for take-off at 4.20 am and headed out towards Dieppe. At the satellite aerodrome at Fairlop, 81 and 154 Squadrons also linked up with the Wing. Unfortunately things on the ground had not gone to plan and the ground troops were beginning to suffer heavy casualties, as German reinforcements arrived to repel the raid; so much so that by 11.00 am, the order was given to withdraw the troops. The RAF was given instructions to lay smoke and cover naval ships and landing craft from attack by German bombers and fighters. Throughout the remainder of the day until around 7.45 pm, the Hornchurch squadrons together with other squadrons in Fighter Command had carried out sortie after sortie over Dieppe and encountered and fought combats with German fighters.

In all the Hornchurch squadrons had destroyed nine enemy aircraft and damaged seven, for the loss of three pilots killed. Although the raid had been a failure, important lessons were learnt and put to good use, when the invasion of Normandy was being planned for 1944.

During September, two new squadrons arrived to take up residence at the aerodrome; these were 350 Squadron, the Belgian Spitfire unit, on the 23rd led by Squadron Leader D.A. Guillaume, who would replace 340 (French) Squadron, who left for Biggin Hill. The Australian Squadron, 453, arrived on 26th September.

The aerodrome was visited by several important dignitaries during October and November, including His Excellency Senior Monir de Arago, the Brazilian Ambassador to the Court of St James who presented two Spitfires to 64 Squadron. 350 Squadron was visited and presented medals by the Belgian Prime Minister in exile, Monsieur Pierlot and a tour of the aerodrome was also laid on for Mr Kanellopoulos, the Deputy Prime Minister and Minister of Defence to the Greek Government. One particular visit of interest was the arrival of a famous Soviet woman sniper, Lieutenant Pavlichenko, who had claimed to have killed more than 300 Germans. She was shown around the various buildings and was taken to the firing butts where she was allowed to climb into a Spitfire and fire off the guns.

With the close of the year, Hornchurch had seen the comings and goings of many squadrons, which were made up of commonwealth or European pilots. The Australians, Belgians, Canadians, Czechoslovakians, French and a few Americans had all fought hard and well against the enemy. Hornchurch had now truly become a multi-national fighter station.

Top: Spitfire Mk Vb AB916 of 313 (Czechoslovak) Squadron at Hornchurch 1942. This aircraft was flown during this time by F/Lt Frantisek Fajtl of A Flight.

Bottom: The Czechs hurry to their aircraft to begin another mission. *(IWM CH 17974)*

Top: Czech pilots of 313 Squadron discuss events following their return from operations over northern France. *(Author)*

Bottom: Czechoslovakian Pilot Officer V. Jicha of 313 Czech Squadron is greeted by his pet dog 'Jara', upon his return from a sortie over enemy-occupied France in 1942. *(IWM CH 5416)*

Top: The Czechs relax and have some fun out at dispersal, by giving one of their pilots the 'bumps'; perhaps it was his birthday. *(IWM CH 17972)*

Bottom: The 1941/42 RAF Hornchurch football team with their display of winners' trophies laid out in front. *(PHC)*

Top: The girls who kept the chaps fed. Staff of the NAAFI canteen stand for the camera with their floral design overalls –1942. *(PHC)*

Bottom: Spitfire BM252 'Bombay City' of 122 Squadron is checked over by her maintenance crew, May 1942. Following her time with 122 Squadron, the aircraft also served with 222, 316 and 130 Squadrons until being struck off charge on 6th September 1945. *(IWM CH 5748)*

Top: Squadron commanders and pilots of the Hornchurch Wing sit for a group photograph during the spring of 1942. Many were aces or on their way to becoming distinguished fighter pilots. Front row from right: Michael Donnet, 3rd F/Lt Don Kingaby, 4th S/Ldr Petrus Hugo, 5th S/Ldr Wilfred Duncan Smith, 6th G/Capt Harry Broadhurst (station commander), 7th W/Cdr Peter Powell, 8th S/Ldr Leon Prevot, 9th F/Lt Jim Hallowes, 11th S/Ldr Eric Thomas. Second row 7th from right: S/Ldr Pat Jameson. *(Broadhurst Collection)*

In May 1942, 27-year-old Flight Sergeant Georges Nadon of 122 Squadron was the subject of a press story following the daily routine of an operational fighter pilot. Nadon was a French Canadian and the article was titled 'A day in the life of a Canadian Flight Sergeant fighter pilot.' The following five photographs were just some of the many taken that day.

A member of the ground crew helps to strap in Flight Sergeant Nadon and makes sure everything is properly adjusted. *(IWM CH 6780)*

Top: Following a sortie, Flight Sergeant Nadon taxies in across the field, while two of the ground crew hold on to the wing tips to steady the aircraft. *(IWM CH 6786)*

Bottom: Immediately after its return from a sweep, the Spitfire is refuelled and any necessary repairs are made. *(IWM CH 6788)*

Top: The NAAFI van makes a very welcome arrival out at dispersal and Flight Sergeant Nadon gets some refreshments from the attendant. *(IWM CH 6789)*

Bottom: As the day closes, Nadon has an off-duty drink at the local pub (The Good Intent Pub?) and enjoys the company of some of the regulars. *(IWM CH 6798)*

A German aerial reconnaissance photo of Hornchurch taken during a bombing raid dated 1942. It clearly shows that the majority of the bombs dropped fell outside the area of the aerodrome, which is located on the left. The buildings (centre left) in the field show Sutton's School. Top of the photograph shows Sutton's Institute and St George's Hospital, while the nearby housing and roads are shown at the bottom. *(National Archive)*

The following sequence of ten photographs was taken at Hornchurch during June 1942 and titled 'All in the Day's work of RAF Fighter Command'. They show the events of an operational sortie and the work carried out by the pilots and ground personnel of 64 and 122 Squadrons.

Top: 'Warming up' a Spitfire MkV of 64 Squadron. Four ground crew, seated on the tail, hold down the aircraft to keep it from nosing over, while the flight mechanic increases the throttle on the 1,000 horsepower Rolls-Royce Merlin engine. *(IWM CH 5753)*

Bottom: Nicknamed 'The Ghost Train' because of the white bicycles they ride. Pilots leave the briefing room after receiving information on their next mission and head for their dispersal points. *(IWM CH 5747)*

Top: An excellent photograph showing some of the flying kit worn by Fighter Command's pilots during 1942. The pilot featured is Michael Donnet, a Belgian who flew with 64 Squadron. He is wearing a G-type oxygen mask, MkIV goggles and C-type flying helmet. *(IWM CH 5755)*

Bottom: Waiting for the call into action. Pilots of 122 Squadron sit at readiness outside their dispersal hut. *(IWM CH 5757)*

Top: Squadron Leader Wilfred Duncan Smith bids farewell to his spaniel pup 'Vicki' before heading out on another sortie leading 64 Squadron over France in June 1942. *(IWM CH 5759)*

Bottom: The emergency fire tender with crew stand ready for immediate call, when the squadrons return. Note fireman with asbestos fire suit. *(IWM)*

After the squadrons return from their missions over enemy occupied Europe, the ground crews immediately begin to refuel and renew the aircraft ready for the next sortie. Here a Spitfire is refuelled from a petrol bowser. *(IWM CH 5773)*

Top: On its return the station engineering officer examines an aircraft of 122 Squadron, which is battle-damaged. He estimates the damage and instructs the repairs to be put in hand at once. *(IWM CH 5777)*

Bottom left: Ammunition is wheeled to the aircraft by the armament squad, who immediately re-arm the Spitfire. *(IWM CH 5778)*

Bottom right: Working the night shift. Aircraft of Hornchurch's squadrons have taken part in two or three sweeps during the day. The maintenance hands work overtime to get as many aircraft ready by dawn the next day. Note the black-out curtains above. *(IWM CH 5784)*

Top: Some of the Erks – ground crew of 64 Squadron pose for a snapshot while seated on the tailplane of a Spitfire. *(PHC)*

Bottom: A wonderful aerial shot of Spitfire MkVs of 81 Squadron, part of the Hornchurch Wing, flying over the Essex countryside in June 1942. 81 Squadron operated from Hornchurch's satellite airfield at Fairlop. *(IWM CH 6378)*

Top: The station commander adjusts his Sidcot flying suit, while his WAAF driver, leading aircraftwoman Mary Ford sorts out the map of the area over which he intends to fly.
(IWM CH 6818)

Bottom: Group Captain Lott talking with a Free French squadron leader of 340 'Ile de France' Squadron before take-off.
(IWM CH 6819)

Top left: Station commander Group Captain Charles George Lott DSO, DFC, receives a telephone call giving him instructions regarding the day's operations against the enemy. Lott took over command of Hornchurch from Harry Broadhurst on 14th May 1942. *(IWM CH 6803)*

Top right: Irish flying ace, Wing Commander Brendan 'Paddy' Finucane DSO, DFC & 2 bars led the Hornchurch Wing briefly between June and mid July, before being killed on the 15th, when his aircraft sank after ditching in the sea, taking him to the bottom of the Channel. His Spitfire had received damage caused by enemy ground fire during an operational sweep. *(F. Decmar)*

Bottom: Belgian Sergeant Pilot L.V. Flohimont from Liège of 350 Squadron stands with his Spitfire 'Yaunde.' The aircraft was one of many presented and paid for by the Belgian Congo. *(IWM CH 6348)*

CHAPTER 6

THE TIDE TURNS
1943 – 1945

At the beginning of January 1943, Hornchurch's station commander, Group Captain George Lott left to take up a new position as Senior Air Staff Officer at 81 Group; his position was temporarily taken over by Wing Commander Bentley until the arrival of a new commanding officer. On 5th January Group Captain A.G Adnams arrived to fill this role.

All squadrons were scrambled on 20th January, when the Germans launched the largest daylight raid they had carried out since the Battle of Britain. Although enemy aircraft were sighted and chased, only 64 Squadron managed to claim one destroyed and two damaged.

In February, a new flightpath extension was opened, which extended from east to west across the South End Road. A new control tower had also been constructed and was sited across the north-south flightpath, opposite the main hangars. This gave the control tower personnel full view of both flightpaths.

On 24th March, American Flying Officer Raimund Sanders Draper of 64 Squadron was tragically killed, while conducting an air-test over the aerodrome, when his aircraft's engine began to falter. Too low to bale out he was forced to make the decision to force land. However, he was confronted with the two school buildings of Sutton's school, which lay in his path. Draper was able to clear the first one, but the second building was far higher. He chose to nose his aircraft down into the playing field between the two buildings and in doing so came to rest hitting the corner of the senior school building. Unfortunately Sanders Draper was killed in the landing. In his brave attempt to miss the school he had saved the lives of many school children who had been at class that day.

March saw a new Wing Commander Flying arrive - Wing Commander John Kilmartin. He had fought with 1 Squadron during the Battle of France and 43 Squadron during 1940. A man of vast experience and leadership qualities.

During this period the Wing was given the role as high altitude escort on bomber raids into France, Belgium and Holland. The squadrons were equipped with the MkIXA Spitfires which had a two-stage supercharger engine giving the aircraft extra boost to 25,000 feet and taking the aircraft up to 30,000 feet. The aircraft were also fitted at this time with jettison fuel tanks, which allowed the squadrons a longer range into enemy territory when escorting the American bombers.

During April, 222 Natal Squadron returned to Hornchurch led by Squadron Leader E.J. Harrington. This was its fourth tour at Hornchurch, having operated from the airfield three times previously in 1940. On 28th June 129 'Mysore' Squadron moved to Hornchurch from Ibsley where it exchanged its old MkVs for Spitfire IXs. Throughout the following months of June, July and August, Hornchurch squadrons continued the important work of protecting the vast bomber raids now doing great damage to the German war machine. The American bomber crews were full of genuine praise for the work, being done by their Spitfire escorts, many saying that they preferred them to the P47 Thunderbolt fighter.

On 8th September, Operation Starkey was put into effect, which would see the increase of bomber and fighter sweeps over the Calais area. This plan had been devised by the Allied Joint Planning Staff whose task it was to convince the enemy that the planned Allied invasion for Europe would take place in and around that area of northern France. The Hornchurch Wing would be heavily involved during raids against marshalling yards, canal barges, troop and ammunition trains or any targets of opportunity. This operation would continue well into 1944.

On 18th October, 485 New Zealand Squadron arrived to start operations working alongside 129 and 222.

1943 saw many visits by dignitaries, including His Highness the Duke of Gloucester, the Regent of Iraq, and two Arabian princes.

In November 66 Squadron moved in briefly to replace 485 Squadron who left for Drem. On 18th December Peter Simpson was appointed as Wing Leader at Hornchurch; he was the last wing leader that the aerodrome would have before the fighter squadrons moved south from Hornchurch in preparation for the invasion of Europe in 1944. 350 Squadron returned for its third tour on 30th December. Hornchurch had played its part in the build up of Fighter Command's preparations against the German defences on the French coast. Now 1944 and the promise of the invasion and liberation of Europe lay ahead.

Top: During February 1943, Sir John Colville, the Governor Designate of Bombay visited the station to meet the pilots of 122 'Bombay' Squadron. Here Sir John (right) is touring the aerodrome accompanied by the station commander Group Captain A.G. Adnams (centre). *(IWM CH 8633)*

Bottom: The pilots of 64 Squadron formed their own football team at Hornchurch and are lined up for the obligatory team photograph before the match. Back row, left to right: Sanders Draper 4th, Clive Mellersh 6th. Front row: George Mason 2nd, Michael Donnet 4th, William Crawford-Compton, 5th and Bob Pulman 6th. Sanders Draper was killed on 24th March 1943, when he crashed his aircraft in an attempt to avoid hitting Sutton's School after it had developed engine failure. *(RAF Hornchurch Association)*

Top: On 5th May 1943, delegates of the Turkish Production Mission arrived at the aerodrome to talk with some of Britain's top-line fighter pilots and inspect aircraft and equipment. The photograph shows Major General Sirri Seyrek, president of the delegation (left) and Mr Imadettin Karacali talking to Squadron Leader Donald Kingaby, DFM & 2 Bars, who had destroyed 21 enemy aircraft. *(IWM CH 8447)*

Bottom: A group photo of the Turkish Production Mission. Left to right: Unknown, Mr N. Artunkai, Major Turagay – Turkish Air Attache, Group Captain Adnams, Mr Celal Imre, Major General Witham (with dark hat), unknown pilot, Major General Sirri Seyrek, S/Ldr Don Kingaby, Mr Salahattin Sanbasoglu, Mr Adil Aktolug, Group Captain Dore and Mr J. Tyler (MOI). *(IWM CH 8448)*

Top: Members of the delegation watch a Spitfire undergo firing tests at the aerodrome's firing butts.
(IWM CH 8455)

Bottom: The men and women of the signals watch pictured at RAF Hornchurch's operations room, which was situated in the Masonic Hall, Romford. Joy York seated in front row, extreme right, served at Hornchurch during 1940, and returned for a second tour in 1943. *(Joy Caldwell)*

Top: The following three photographs were taken on 23rd April 1943, when a Spitfire was presented to 122 Squadron by the Governor of Bermuda, Viscount Knollys, accompanied by Admiral Harcourt. The aircraft named 'Spithead Billy' was a gift of Mr William Frith, a citizen of Bermuda. Mr Frith not only bought the aircraft, but also provided an allowance for the pilot when on leave. Here Viscount Knollys is presenting a cheque for the Spitfire to Pilot Officer E. R. Burnard who hailed from Hamilton, Bermuda. *(IWM CH 9859)*

Bottom: The Governor of Bermuda unveiling 'Spithead Billy'. *(IWM CH 9863)*

Top: Viscount Knollys talking to Pilot Officer Burnard in front of the presentation Spitfire. *(IWM CH 9861)*

Bottom: Wing Commander John Ratten was the first Australian officer to be promoted to wing commander rank and then lead a wing in Fighter Command. He was appointed Wing Commander Flying at Hornchurch on 7th May 1943. Pictured in his Spitfire MkIX, the aircraft carries the name of his wife as well as a New Zealand charm. The sign of the 'Saint' is also visible. *(IWM CH 10049)*

Top: Spitfire MkIX MH434 is prepared for another mission on escort duty over northern France. The aircraft is seen wearing the code letters of 222 Natal Squadron, which was based at Hornchurch between August and November 1943. The Spitfire arrived at Hornchurch on 19th August and was flown by South African pilot and flight commander Henry Lardner-Burke, who christened it 'Mylcraine'. The name was duly painted beneath the left side of the cockpit. Lardner-Burke claimed three enemy aircraft whilst flying MH434. It survived the war and is now owned and flown by Ray Hanna of The Old Flying Machine Company Collection at the Imperial War Museum, Duxford. *(Bill Burge via Peter Arnold Collection)*

Bottom: On 6th October 1943, a Spitfire aircraft was presented to 129 'Mysore' Squadron, when the Uruguayan Chargé d'Affaires, Senor Montero de Bustamante arrived at the aerodrome at 11 am to unveil the aircraft. The Spitfire was the 16th aircraft to be paid for by the people of Uruguay. The photograph shows Senor Bustamante speaking before the unveiling. On his right is the Right Honourable Harold Balfour MP, the Under Secretary of State for Air and Air Vice-Marshal H.W. L Saunders, centre is Air Vice-Marshal Roderic Hill. *(IWM CH 11386)*

Top: F/Lt Arthur 'Joe' Leigh, DFM, DFC, of 129 'Mysore' Squadron with his ground crew in September 1943. 'Joe' was flying a presentation Spitfire named 'Kamba Meru.' *(A.C. Leigh)*

Bottom: 'Uruguay XVI' of 129 Squadron undertakes a flypast over the aerodrome after the unveiling ceremony. *(IWM CH 11391)*

Top: New Zealand pilots of 485 Squadron at Hornchurch in October 1943. Left to right: P/O J.G. Dasent, P/O D.A. Roberts and F/Lt K.C Lee. Dasent was killed in a flying accident on 22nd November 1944, when his Spitfire's engine failed over the Firth of Forth and he was unable to bale out and was drowned after ditching into the sea. *(Sports & General)*

Bottom: The Duke of Gloucester arrived at Hornchurch on 26th October 1943 to present 164 Argentine Squadron with their new squadron badge. This photograph shows the guard of honour, the RAF Regiment being inspected by His Royal Highness. *(IWM CH 11432)*

Top: One of the many Spitfires that were publicly funded during the war. This aircraft named 'Royal Eltham' and 'New Eltham' was handed over to 485 New Zealand Squadron at Hornchurch on 30th October 1943. Posing with the aircraft for the official photograph is F/Lt K.C. Lee. *(Author)*

Bottom: Hornchurch was again asked to host a royal visit on 15th November 1943, when the Regent of Iraq, Emir Abdullah Illah paid the aerodrome a visit as part of his tour of this country. The Regent of Iraq pictured centre, is shown around the aerodrome by station commander, Wing Commander David Scott-Malden (left) accompanied by senior intelligence officer Squadron Leader D.S. Franze (right). *(IWM CH 11606)*

Top: On 22nd November, the Arabian Princes Emir Feisal and Emir Khalid were also guests at the station. Here they are seen being shown a fighter pilot's dinghy in the parachute store. *(IWM CH 11669)*

Bottom: 222 Natal Squadron was presented with two Spitfires on 25th November 1943, by His Excellency Senor Don Guillermo de Blanck, the Cuban Ambassador. The Spitfires were funded by the British community in Cuba. The aircraft were named 'Cuba Libra' and 'Spirit of Marti.' Here the Cuban minister is unveiling one of the aircraft. *(IWM CH 11731)*

Top: 222 Squadron Flying Officer R.F. Bass from Bolton, Lancashire, with his new aircraft 'Cuba Libra' after the hand-over ceremony at Hornchurch. *(IWM CH 11733)*

Bottom: June 1944 saw the men of 207 Flight, 55 Maintenance Repair Unit stationed at Hornchurch to undertake repair work caused by German V1 rockets. Seen here with one of their lorries and unit badge. *(H. Bullock)*

Singalese cadets from Ceylon and Jamaica at Hornchurch in 1944, during their training for aircrew duties. Cadet L.Vanden Driesen from Bambalapitiya, Colombo, climbs into the cockpit of a trainer aircraft. *(IWM CH 12078)*

CHAPTER 7

POSTWAR TO PRESENT

The general duties and running of the aerodrome remained virtually the same over the next few years. An aviation candidate selection board was opened in January 1947, but within a month had closed down due to a major fuel crisis that had swept across Britain owing to another severe winter. Good news did arrive in the spring, when Hornchurch was selected for the new Officers' Advanced Training School, which remained at Hornchurch until August 1948.

Flying returned to the aerodrome with the formation of 86 Reserve Centre in May 1948. The centre's job was to keep up the standard of flying and navigation competence for the many ex-RAF gentlemen, who had re-enlisted into the RAF Volunteer Reserve. Also that year 17 Reserve Flying School was formed and operated by the Shorts Aircraft Company. The flying school had Tiger Moth and Chipmunk aircraft and also twin-engine types, the Avro Anson and Airspeed Oxford.

In October 1949, it was decided that the RAF Combined Selection Centre was to be moved from North Weald to Hornchurch. The aerodrome opened its doors to the first candidates on 25th October. In November, Hornchurch had been in existence for over 30 years which meant it was qualified to be awarded a station badge.

During the year of 1949, Hornchurch was heavily involved in the accommodation of service personnel and transport used to keep the docks and power stations running, when a number of serious strikes hit Britain. Emergency labour units were set up and 1,310 men were billeted within hangars and tented accommodation inside the camp.

Throughout the 1950s, Hornchurch continued with its role as the RAF's Aircrew Selection Centre and opened its gates to the public annually with its Battle of Britain 'At Home' air displays. Short Brothers finally lost the contract for the 17 Reserve Flying School in 1952, but the company Aerowork took over the contract to operate 1 Civilian Anti-Aircraft Co-operation Unit, which operated Avro Oxfords, two Mosquito and two Spitfire aircraft, used for communication. During the 'Great Flood' of 1953, when tidal flooding washed over Norfolk, Canvey Island, etc; Hornchurch was again used to accommodate RAF personnel sent to help with constructing breakwaters to hold back the flooding.

During the later part of the 1950s, Hornchurch's duties were gradually being cut back, as was its personnel, but 1959 brought some new arrivals, when a detachment from the RAF Balloon Unit arrived to set up static balloon jump training for the Special Air Service (TA). One of the army units that used this facility was 289 Parachute Light Regiment, Royal Horse Artillery (TA).

By 1960, the Aircrew Selection Centre had seen a vast drop in candidates due to National Service coming to a close. That September saw the last air display held at the aerodrome. The event was organised by the Joint League of Friends of Romford, Hornchurch and Dagenham Hospitals. A crowd of over 20,000 attended the show, to witness a marvellous display of low-flying aerobatics.

On 9th April 1962, the Aircrew Selection Centre closed its doors for the last time after 14 years of testing candidates for the Royal Air Force, but the station maintained a small holding party to upkeep the buildings. The closure of the aerodrome now seemed set and on 1st July 1962, the inevitable happened when it became official.

The following year in February, the Air Ministry put Hornchurch up for sale by auction which was conducted by estate agents Kemsley, Whitely and Ferris of Romford. The main area of the flightpath was leased to the Hoveringham Gravel Company to excavate, but all the main buildings and hangars were to be demolished. By 1966, the bulldozers and demolition contractors had achieved what the Luftwaffe had failed to do during WW2.

A housing estate was built around the remains of RAF Hornchurch and a new school was constructed using the parade ground as its play area, the school being named the R.J. Mitchell School, after the designer of the Spitfire aeroplane. Today many of the roads bear the names of famous pilots who flew from Hornchurch, men like Alan Deere, (Deere Avenue), 'Sailor' Malan (Malan Square), William Crawford-Compton (Crawford-Compton Close) Harry Broadhurst (Broadhurst Way) and so on.

After final gravel extraction had been completed in 1979, The London Borough of Havering set aside 160 acres of old aerodrome land to be turned into a country park, which still had a few remains from wartime, including pill boxes, gun emplacements and a single Blenheim dispersal pen. Today the country park is used for casual walking, joggers and wildlife enthusiasts and maintained by a team of professional and dedicated rangers, who organise tours of the country park to discuss the aerodrome's auspicious past.

Hornchurch's history was also kept alive through the establishment of The RAF Hornchurch Association in 1983, by a group of volunteers who wanted to display artefacts and memorabilia related to the aerodrome. The idea of forming a group was the brainchild of the late Mr Ted Exall and they still hold exhibitions regularly.

At present the only permanent display of Sutton's Farm and RAF Hornchurch memorabilia in the country is held within the Hornchurch Wing Collection at the Purfleet Heritage & Military Centre, where you will find an incredible array of photographs, artefacts, uniforms, Zeppelin relics and aircraft remains from the Battle of Britain period.

The aerodrome's past received further publicity in April 2003, when a TV programme was scheduled by the 'Two Men in a Trench' archaeologist team, who excavated parts of the airfield and interviewed veterans from the Battle of Britain.

The history of RAF Hornchurch is still deeply rooted within the proud people of Hornchurch and its environs and their role during some of Britain's darkest hours. The airmen, who day after day continued to climb into the skies against the enemy, to keep our country free from tyranny, should always be remembered. I hope this book will always serve as a reminder to you of them and their sacrifice.

Top: Officers and cadets of 2048 (Dagenham) Squadron, Air Training Corps, at Hornchurch during a visit in 1946. *(No. 2048 Dagenham ATC Squadron)*

Bottom: A Chipmunk trainer of 17 Reserve Flying School stands ready in front of the main hangar at Hornchurch −1951. *(D. Bendon)*

Top: The altar inside the RAF Hornchurch station church of St Michael's and All Angels – 10th March 1952. *(National Archives)*

Bottom: A Tiger Moth biplane belonging to the 17 Reserve Flying School, is refuelled in front of the main hangar by David Bendon, who worked for Short Brothers & Harland in 1952. *(D. Bendon)*

Hornchurch aerodrome as it was in the early 1950s. *(National Archives)*

Top left: Bomb disposal 1953 – men of 6226 Bomb Disposal Flight arrived at Hornchurch during that year and carried out work on hundreds of wartime munitions, both German and Allied. This work was carried out not far from the aerodrome at what was known as the bomb cemetery, located near Gerpins Lane, Rainham. This photograph shows the procedure of steaming out TNT from a bomb. *(D. Kilgariff)*

Top right: The result of applying a match to a large amount of TNT, after steaming out the contents of various sized bombs. *(D. Kilgariff)*

Bottom: Men of 6226 (BD) Flight pose for a snap alongside one of three German V1 'Doodlebug' rockets that were stored at Hornchurch. Left to right: Sgt Rhys Hopkins, Danny Kilgariff and Cpl Ian Smith. *(D. Kilgariff)*

Top: Hornchurch's famous dog mascot 'Binder,' who had remained at the aerodrome following the war. He had been 'Paddy' Finucane's canine companion during 1940. Binder is pictured in the canteen. *(RAF Hornchurch Association)*

Middle: A boxing tournament at Hornchurch. The sports event took place on the evening of Thursday 4th February 1954 and this photograph shows a lightweight bout between LAC Byrne and Corporal Cox. *(J. Cox)*

Bottom: Drivers of the RAF Motor Transport Section line up proudly with their cars – 1954. *(J. Cox)*

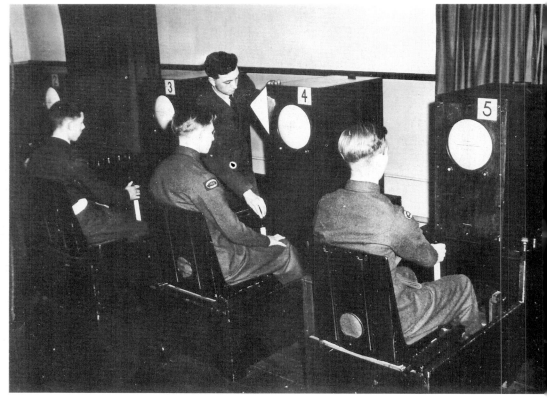

Top: New arrivals to Hornchurch's Aircrew Selection Centre arrive by RAF coach and are booked in by a sergeant instructor. *(Air Historical Branch)*

Bottom: Future pilots? Young hopefuls are put through a series of aptitude tests while at the Aircrew Selection Centre. *(Air Historical Branch)*

Another test is undertaken as an instructor looks on. *(Air Historical Branch)*

Top: Air cadets of Malvern College are given a close-up inspection of one of Hornchurch's last Spitfires by one of the RAF instructors. *(Air Historical Branch)*

Bottom: View across the aerodrome from one of the E-pens with blockhouse buildings and fire tower in the distance. *(H. La Roche)*

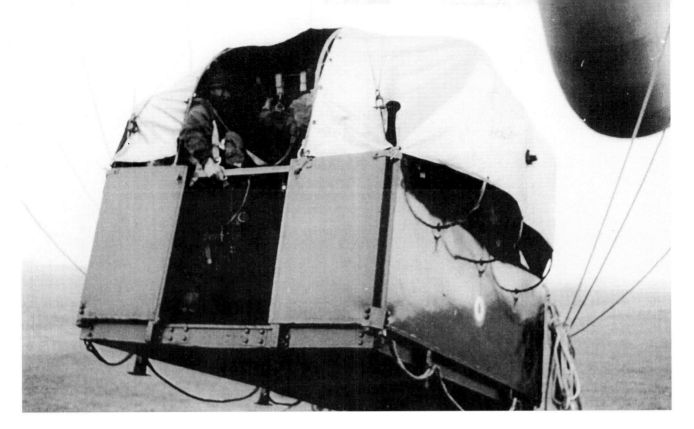

Top: Parachuting at Hornchurch? In February 1959, a RAF balloon unit was sent to Hornchurch to set up static balloon jump training. The photograph shows the balloon cage in which the men of 289 Parachute Light Regiment Territorial Army Reservists will jump, as it starts to slowly rise, attached to a very large barrage balloon. The height for standard practice jumps was 800 feet. *(R.Little)*

Bottom: Safely down! One of the parachutists makes a perfect landing. Notice the instructor with hand-held megaphone. *(R. Little)*

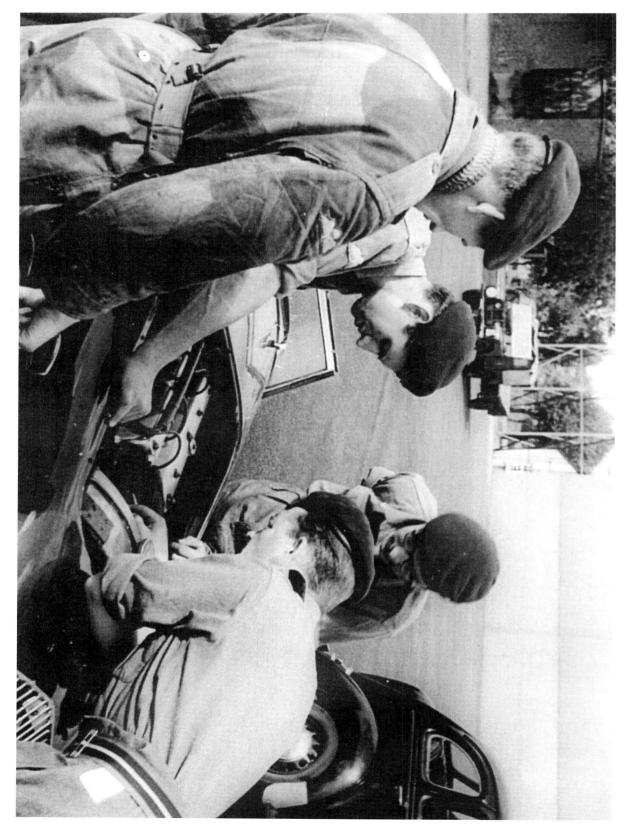

That ought to fix it! Men of 289 Parachute Light Regiment, stationed at Hornchurch in 1959, take time out to do some important car maintenance. *(R. Little)*

Top: Hornchurch's Spitfire MkXIV with ATC cadets in attendance. To the left can be seen a Slingsby Cadet glider belonging to the 614 ATC Gliding School. *(H. La Roche)*

Bottom: Another view of the Spitfire MkXIV parked out on the concrete apron. *(H. La Roche)*

Top: The Spitfire is pushed back off the grass area. Note the barrage balloon used for static parachute jumping. *(J. Cox)*

Bottom: An Arrow Active MkII biplane prepares to take off during Hornchurch's last air display on 3rd September 1960. The aircraft was flown by Mr C. Nepean-Bishop. *(Author)*

Top: A view of the large crowd, which attended the last air display at Hornchurch, with low flying aircraft giving them a thrilling display. *(RAF Hornchurch Association)*

Bottom: Photograph taken by John Cox, a visitor to the last air display, showing the aerobatics that day. *(John Cox)*

Top: Memories of past glories. Hornchurch's Battle of Britain heroes visited the aerodrome in 1960 and were filmed and interviewed for a television production titled 'An English Summer'. The TV play had been written by Hornchurch's operations room controller Ronald Adam. Left to right: Ronald Adam, Group Captain Colin Gray, Group Captain Ronald 'Ras' Berry, Wing Commander Robert Stanford Tuck, TV director, and Group Captain Norman Ryder. *(A.C. Deere)*

Bottom: A great aerial shot of the aerodrome shows its layout prior to it being sold off at auction. At the time of this photograph the aerodrome was being used by the Ford Motor Company at Dagenham as a storage overflow facility. Note all the cars parked around the three hangars. *(Author)*

The main hangar stands empty and awaits its fate. *(R. Ballard)*

Block houses ready for demolition as mother nature begins to take hold – 1963. *(R. Ballard)*

Top: The Guard Room at Hornchurch waits its turn to be destroyed.
(RAF Hornchurch Association)

Bottom: Demolition teams achieve what the Luftwaffe failed to do in 1940, as one of the Hornchurch hangars begins to be knocked down.
(R. Ballard)

Top: On 5th July 1983, a memorial stone was unveiled within the grounds of the R.J. Mitchell School, where once stood RAF Hornchurch. The photograph taken just after the unveiling shows from left to right: Air Chief Marshal Sir Harry Broadhurst, Air Vice-Marshal Kenneth Hayr, ATC cadets of 1838-452 Squadrons, Mr Ted Exall, who organised the memorial fund and Squadron Leader Henryck Szczesny who flew with 74 Squadron during 1940. *(Author)*

Bottom: One of the defensive tett turrets that still lie in position around the remains of the perimeter track of the aerodrome. *(Author)*

154

Top: One of only two pill boxes that remain standing today. *(Author)*

Bottom: Although it looks similar to a pill box, this defensive position could only be entered by underground tunnel and would have been a formidable position to attack, if the Germans had invaded. *(Author)*

Top: The last remaining dispersal pen, now used as a car park within the Hornchurch Country Park. *(Author)*

Bottom: A view across the Hornchurch Country Park today. This shot was taken as a comparison to the photograph taken in 1940 of 222 Squadron Spitfires at dispersal by Joe Crawshaw with St George's Hospital chimney pictured to the right (see page 80). *(Author)*

Top: The infamous St George's laundry chimney still stands today, but is somewhat shorter. During the war it caused a few problems for inexperienced pilots when taking off or landing. *(Author)*

Bottom: The grave headstone of Flying Officer Raimund Sanders Draper of 64 Squadron, who sacrificed his life on 24th March 1943 so that others might live. *(B. Green)*

Top: The Officers' Mess still stands today and is located in Astra Close. It is now used as a medical centre. *(Author)*

Bottom: The Good Intent public house situated in the South End Road, sited just next to the aerodrome, was one of the local pubs where pilots and ground personnel would go for a beer. *(Author)*

Top: The pub sign for the Good Intent – a Spitfire diving into attack. *(Author)*

Bottom: In April 2003, the country park was visited by archaeologists in order to make a TV documentary about RAF Hornchurch's role during the Battle of Britain. The programme, entitled 'Two Men in a Trench', showed the team uncovering various remains of the airfield and some RAF personnel items were recovered including part of a pilot's goggles. Here the team are filming by an excavated tett turret. *(Author).*

SELECT BIBLIOGRAPHY

The following books are of interest to those wishing to know more about the history of Sutton's Farm and RAF Hornchurch:

Hornchurch Scramble, Richard C. Smith, Grub Street 2000

Hornchurch Offensive, Richard C. Smith, Grub Street 2001

Hornchurch Eagles, Richard C. Smith, Grub Street 2002

Al Deere, Wartime Fighter Pilot-Peacetime Commander, Richard C. Smith, Grub Street 2003

Nine Lives, A/Cdr Alan Deere, Wingham Press Ltd 1992

Richard Hillary, David M. Ross, Grub Street 2000

Stapme, David M. Ross, Grub Street 2002

The Greatest Squadron of Them All – The History of 603 Squadron Vol 1 & 2
David M. Ross et al, Grub Street 2003

The Last Enemy, Richard Hillary, Macmillan & Co Ltd 1942

First Things First, Eric Smith, Ian Henry Publications Ltd 1992

Raiders Approach, S/Ldr H.T. Sutton, Gale & Polden 1956

Fly for your Life, Larry Forrester, Frederick Muller Ltd 1956

Spitfire into Battle, G/Capt W. Duncan Smith, John Murray Ltd 1981